Timekeeping

Explore the History and Science of Telling Time

with 15 projects

LINDA FORMICHELLI & W. ERIC MARTIN

Illustrated by Sam Carbaugh

~ Latest Titles in the *Build It Yourself* Series ~

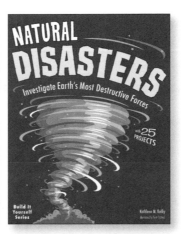

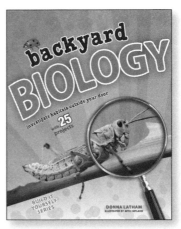

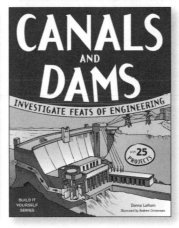

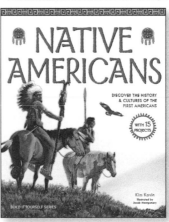

Check out more titles on www.nomadpress.net

Nomad Press is committed to preserving ancient forests and natural resources. We elected to print *Timekeeping: Explore the History and Science of Telling Time* on 4,007 lbs. of Williamsburg Recycled 30% offset.

Nomad Press made this paper choice because our printer, Sheridan Books, is a member of Green Press Initiative, a nonprofit program dedicated to supporting authors, publishers, and suppliers in their efforts to reduce their use of fiber obtained from endangered forests.

For more information, visit **www.greenpressinitiative.org**.

This book was manufactured by Sheridan Books,
Ann Arbor, MI USA.
November 2012, Job #341843
ISBN: 978-1-61930-136-8

Illustrations by Sam Carbaugh
Educational Consultant Marla Conn

Questions regarding the ordering of this book should be addressed to
Independent Publishers Group
814 N. Franklin St., Chicago, IL 60610
www.ipgbook.com

Nomad Press
2456 Christian St.
White River Junction, VT 05001
www.nomadpress.net

Contents

TIMELINE

4000 BCE:	The first Egyptian calendars appear depicting the flood, seed, and harvest seasons, each four lunar months long.
3000 BCE:	Egyptians change to a 365-day calendar with 12 months of 30 days each, plus five extra days at the end.
1400 BCE:	Egyptians start using the clepsydra water clock to keep time.
750 BCE:	Romulus, the founder of Rome, creates a 304-day calendar. It is later changed to a 355-day calendar, and then a calendar that alternates between 355, 378, 355, and 379 days every four years!
560 BCE:	Anaximander introduces the sundial into Greece.
200–50 BCE:	The giant Tower of the Winds water clock is built in Athens, Greece.
45 BCE:	Julius Caesar changes the Roman calendar to what is known as the Julian calendar, putting January and February at the beginning of the year. The number of days of each month is 30 or 31, except February, which has 29, and 30 every fourth year.
8 BCE:	The Roman senate steals a day from February to make August and July the same length. This keeps Roman Emperor Augustus Caesar happy.
700–1000:	The Chinese begin using clepsydras powered by waterwheels.
1090:	Su Sung's water clock is completed in China. It measures over 30 feet tall (9 meters). The clock is stolen in 1126.
mid-1200s:	The idea for a mechanical escapement first appears in the sketchbooks of French architect Villard de Honnecourt.
mid-1300s:	Clockmakers discover how to use separate gears to count off hours.
1392:	A mechanical clock designed by Italian Giovanni de Dondi is built in Wells Cathedral. It includes figures of knights that joust every hour.
1500:	Clocks are made small enough that wealthy Europeans begin buying them for their homes.
1500–1510:	German locksmith Peter Henlein replaces heavy weights with springs to drive the gears of a clock.
1525:	Jacob Zech of Prague invents a spiral pulley to smooth out the movement of a clock's mainspring.
1582:	Pope Gregory XIII of Rome introduces the Gregorian calendar to deal with the extra time that has accumulated in the Julian calendar. He takes the extra leap day out of century years not divisible by 400. This is the calendar we use today.

1637: Galileo designs a pendulum clock that he never has a chance to build.

1656: Dutch scientist Christian Huygens builds the first pendulum clock, unaware of Galileo's design.

1675: King Charles II founds the Royal Observatory in Greenwich, England, to track the sun, moon, and planets in order to create accurate star catalogs for British ships to sail safely around the world.

1772: John Harrison of England is recognized for inventing a chronometer accurate enough for sailors to tell where they are on the ocean within a half-degree of longitude.

1808: William Congreve invents a rolling ball clock using interlocking gears.

1847: The British government passes a law requiring all railroads to use Greenwich Mean Time.

1880: Pierre and Jacques Curie discover that quartz crystals vibrate at a constant rate when an electric current is run through them.

1883: The United States implements a system of time zones proposed by Charles Dowd. The following year, 25 countries meet to create a system of global time zones, with each zone measured from the prime meridian.

1916: The first official daylight saving time is observed in Germany and Austria. The United States passes its first daylight saving law in 1918.

late 1930s: More accurate quartz crystal clocks are made, but they remain large and expensive.

1949: The first atomic clock is built. It is 10 times more accurate than a quartz clock.

1964: The first computerized timing device is used in the Olympics in Tokyo, Japan.

1970s: Digital quartz wristwatches become popular, thanks to quartz designs that run on less power.

1978–1993: GPS satellites are launched.

2007: The United States changes daylight savings to start the second Sunday in March and end the first Sunday in November.

2010: The official U.S. Government time is set to an atomic clock so accurate it will not be off by a second in over 100 million years.

Now Is the Time

Time is a funny thing. We keep time, save time, lose time, buy time, and make time when we're running late. People ask if we have the time, and we answer them as if we do. We talk about time as if it's something we can touch and feel, but of course time isn't like that at all.

First 10, Then 15

Try to imagine a world without time. You'd be 10 years old, 5 years old, 41 years old, and newly born all at once. Night and day, winter and summer—would all happen together, and you would get very, very confused. Your teacher might accuse you of not handing in your homework, while you'd be sure that you did. Oddly, you would both be correct!

We can't point to time or put it on a leash to take it for a walk. But we can keep track of time just by looking at the world around us. The earth spins, and the sun rises and sets. The seasons change, and your hair grows longer. Running water wears away rock, and an egg in a frying pan cooks over heat.

Things change in the world, and we want to know how long these changes take.

When will the weather turn warm again? When will you arrive at school if you leave the house when the sun is rising? How long do you have to wait before you can eat that egg?

Timekeeping: Explore the History and Science of Telling Time explores how people have always used the changing world to track time. It will have you using tools and supplies from around your house to make lots of fun projects, including clocks similar to those used long ago. Time can be a tricky topic, but by the end of this book, you should have a handle on it—if time could have a handle in the first place, that is.

THE BIRTH OF TIME

Imagine that on a school field trip your class gets lost in the woods or stranded on an island in the Pacific Ocean. You have nothing with you except the clothes on your back and the sandwiches in your backpacks. No cell phones, no watches, no modern tools of any kind. What do you do?

Timekeeping

This might seem scary, but the first humans lived like this for thousands of years. Without hotels, supermarkets, and refrigerators, they lived in caves and hunted their own food. Over time they learned to build their own shelters and grow their own crops. As the seasons changed they followed herds of animals that moved across the land. To prepare for winter, they made coats from animal pelts and smoked meat to eat.

dawn: when the sun rises above the **horizon**.

horizon: the point in the distance where the sky and the earth (or the sea) seem to meet.

dusk: when the sun dips below the horizon.

new moon: when the sun, earth, and moon are lined up, with the moon in the middle. The side of the moon lit by the sun is facing away from Earth so the moon is not visible.

Long ago, time was much simpler than it is today.

Seconds, hours, weeks, months—none of these existed. The only units of time were those that people could track with the naked eye. A day was made up of **dawn**, noon, and **dusk**, which means there were no "nine-to-five jobs" or "five o'clock shadows"!

The night sky marked the passage of time, and humans learned to track the moon through its phases. As **new moon** followed new moon, the seasons changed, and as the seasons passed, the height of the noon sun rose and fell.

Over 20,000 years ago, European hunters made an early effort at timekeeping. They scratched lines and made holes in bones and sticks. Experts think these marks were made to record the phases of the moon, from the new moon to the crescent moon to the full moon and back again. With this simple beginning, the first calendar was born.

BCE: put after a date, BCE stands for Before the Common Era and counts down to zero. CE stands for Common Era and counts up from zero. These non-religious terms correspond to BC and AD.

lunar month: the time from one new moon to the next.

lunar calendar: a calendar based on the phases of the moon.

The moon remained our most important "clock" for thousands of years. The first Egyptian calendars, made before 4000 **BCE**, had three seasons (flood, seed, and harvest) that each lasted four **lunar months**. The length of a month was either 28 or 29 days, depending on exactly how long it took the moon to cycle from one new moon to the next.

But keeping track of time with a **lunar calendar** doesn't work. The movement of the moon around the earth, which takes 28 or 29 days, has no relation to the 365¼ days it takes the earth to journey around the sun.

Early Muslim and Hebrew lunar calendars both contained 354 days. This meant that the first day of each year occurred at a different time of the year because Earth had not yet made it all the way around the sun.

To solve the problem of years that were too short, the Egyptian and Hebrew calendars added an extra month every second or third year. Kind of like a leap month!

ANCIENT EGYPTIAN CALENDAR

FLOOD

SEED

HARVEST

ANCIENT HEBREW CALENDAR

30	29	30	29
30	29	30	29 or 30
30	29	30	29 or 30

+ Leap Month

Around 3000 BCE, the Egyptians noticed that Sothis, the star we call Sirius or the Dog Star today, rose next to the sun every 365 days. This happened just before the annual flooding of the Nile. So the Egyptians realized their lunar calendar wasn't quite right. They created a new calendar of 12 months with 30 days each. Then, they added five extra days to the end of the year to create a more accurate 365-day calendar.

In later years, Egyptians explained the origin of the five **epagomenal days** by saying that the god Thoth won them in a dice game played against the moon. Too bad Thoth couldn't try his luck in Vegas!

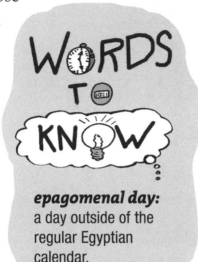

WORDS TO KNOW

epagomenal day: a day outside of the regular Egyptian calendar.

MAKING OUR MODERN CALENDAR

The calendar we use today seems especially stable—30 days has September, April, June, and November. But getting there took a lot of work.

Around 750 BCE, Romulus, the founder of Rome, is believed to have created a 10-month calendar that included six months of 30 days (April, June, Sextilis, September, November, and December) and four months of 31 days (March, May, Quintilis, and October). A few minutes with a calculator tells us this year had only 304 days, which is far too short!

The second king of Rome, Numa Pompilius, tried to correct the problem by adding January and February to the end of the year. The lengths of the months were changed so that half had 29 days and half had 30. Now we're getting closer—354 days. Since the Romans thought that even numbers were unlucky, they added an extra day to make the calendar 355 days long.

As the years passed, the Romans realized that their calendar was still too short. To solve the problem, they added the month of Mercedinus between the 23rd and 24th of February. But the month lasted either 22 or 23 days and was only added every other year. So over a four-year period, the Romans had years lasting 355, 378, 355, and 379 days. Quite complicated!

It's too bad the Romans didn't know about the calendar of the Egyptians.

A Different Kind of Calendar

The Maya **civilization**, which lasted for about 4,000 years in Central America, kept two calendars. One was the standard 365-day **solar calendar**, called *haab*. The other was a 260-day calendar called *tzolkin*, or the "count of the days."

The *tzolkin* was based partly on the movement of the planet Venus, but the number 260 was also important for other reasons. It is about how many days a woman is pregnant before giving birth. Also, 260 is the number you get when you multiply the number of digits on a human's hands and feet (20) with the number of layers in Maya heaven (13).

The Maya used their two calendars at the same time, and together these calendars created a cycle of 18,980 days. This 52-year-long cycle was about how long people lived at the time.

Why did the Romans create an appearing and disappearing month instead of adding 10 days to the calendar? No one knows, but tradition may have won out over common sense. Why do we use a 60-second minute and a 60-minute hour when we count almost everything else by tens? Why 24 hours in a day and not 20 or 30? The answer in each case is tradition. It's often easier to do what's familiar than it is to try something new.

Luckily for us, Julius Caesar was willing to take a risk. When he came to power in 46 BCE, he found that previous government officials had changed the Roman calendar so many times that it was 90 days off from the actual seasons.

WORDS TO KNOW

civilization: a community of people that is advanced in art, science, and government.

solar calendar: a calendar based on how long the earth takes to revolve around the sun.

To get the calendar back on track, Julius declared that the current year (45 BCE) would last 445 days instead of 355. He changed January and February to be the first two months of the year instead of the last. And months would last either 30 or 31 days, except for February, which would have 29 days most of the time and 30 days every fourth year.

To honor Julius, the Roman senate took the month of Quintilis and renamed it July. In 8 BCE, the senate made Sextilis into August to honor the ruler Augustus Caesar. At the same time, they stole a day from February to make August last as long as July. A good idea since Augustus was still in charge at the time!

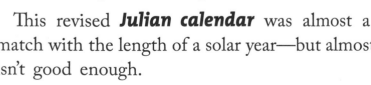

WORDS TO KNOW

Julian calendar: the calendar created by Julius Caesar in 45 BCE.

You can still see signs of the old Roman calendar in the months September, October, November, and December. Sept-, oct-, non-, and deca- are prefixes based on the Latin and Greek words for seven, eight, nine, and ten. Think of the eight-legged octopus, or the decathlon, a track-and-field contest with 10 events. November and December used to be the ninth and tenth months, but when Julius moved January and February, the "novem" and "decem" parts no longer made sense.

This revised **Julian calendar** was almost a match with the length of a solar year—but almost isn't good enough.

equinox: the day in spring (March 20, 21, or 22) or fall (September 20, 21, or 22) when the number of hours of daylight and nighttime are equal everywhere in the world. The sun rises directly in the east and sets directly in the west, everywhere in the world.

Gregorian calendar: the calendar introduced by Pope Gregory XIII as a modification to the Julian calendar.

The calendar was 11 minutes and 14 seconds too long. Eleven minutes might not seem like much, but in 400 years that extra time adds up to three days.

By the year 1582, the spring **equinox** had moved forward 10 days, from March 21 to March 11. This upset the Christian church since the date of Easter each year had been defined as the first Sunday after the first full moon after the spring equinox.

If something wasn't done, Easter would eventually fall on the same day as Christmas.

As Julius Caesar had done 1,600 years earlier, Pope Gregory XIII decided to change the length of the year just once to get the calendar back on track. He decreed that October 4 would be followed by October 15. There would still be a leap year every four years, except that century years divisible by 100, like 2100, would not contain the extra day. Only century years divisible by 400, like 2400, would be leap years. This **Gregorian calendar** that we use now takes care of the 11 extra minutes each year.

Did You Know?

When England switched to the Gregorian calendar in 1752, the calendar jumped from October 4 to October 15. Workers rioted, claiming they had lost 10 days of pay. It's true they weren't paid for those 10 days, but they didn't work those 10 days either.

Will our calendar prevent the solar year from shifting in the future? In fact, our calendar contains 2½ extra days over a 10,000-year period. Thankfully, we can let our great-great-great-(repeat this a hundred times)-grandchildren worry about this when they're rocketing from planet to planet in their personalized spaceships. For the next 2,000 years or so, we're all set.

Is A Better Calendar Possible?

The Gregorian calendar matches the solar year and is used around the world. But it has problems. Most businesses and governments issue reports every three months. But the first quarter of the year (the months January, February, and March) has 90 or 91 days, the second quarter has 91 days, and the final two quarters have 92. The different lengths can make it hard to compare reports from one quarter to the next. Another sore point is that dates don't match the same day of the week from one year to the next. If the Fourth of July is on a Monday this year, next year it will be on Tuesday—unless it's a leap year, in which case it will be on Wednesday!

Many people have offered new calendars that avoid these problems. The most well known was the World Calendar, created in 1834 by Marco Mastrofini. Each quarter has 91 days, with a month of 31 days being followed by two months of 30 days. Since 7 divides evenly into 91, each date would always fall on the same day of the week. Four quarters of 91 days adds up to only 364. World Day would come between December 30 and January 1. Leap Day would come after June 30 every fourth year. These holidays would not be associated with Monday, Tuesday, or any other day.

HMM...

The World Calendar makes sense but probably won't replace the Gregorian calendar we've used for the past 400 years. How many airplane schedules, school records, appointment books, and millions of other documents would have to be changed?

Do you want to be in charge of that?

Marco Mastrofini

ACTIVITY

READING SEASONS FROM A SHADOW

Each day the sun appears to move across the sky from east to west (actually the sun stays in place and the earth spins on its axis). Although the sun may seem to rise and set at the same spot on the horizon each day, the path it takes between those two points varies over the course of the year.

Supplies

- pebbles
- straight stick to push into the ground or flagpole

To learn how the path of the sun changes over the year, you can indirectly observe its changing *arc*. The movement of shadows across the ground shows which season it is.

PUT STICK IN A SUNNY SPOT

PLANT!

1 On a sunny day, go out early in the morning and place a pebble at the end of the stick's (or flagpole's) shadow. Every hour or so throughout the day, place another pebble to mark the end of the shadow. Make sure to place a pebble at noon when the shadow is at its shortest.

2 At day's end, what shape does your row of pebbles form? If it's an arc that curves toward the stick, then the season is summer. If the arc curves away from the stick, it's winter. And if the row of pebbles forms a straight line, then it's either spring or autumn. To find out which, create a new line of pebbles one day each week until the line bends either toward or away from the stick.

USE ROCKS TO TRACK THE SHADOW

NUDGE

3 This experiment will work in many locations in the **Northern Hemisphere** and **Southern Hemisphere**. On or near the **equator**, the sun passes directly overhead twice a year, and the sun's shadow will pass right through the stick. In June, the shadow will arc to the south because the sun is north of the equator. In December, the shadow will arc the other way.

4 If you live way up in Alaska you'll have a different kind of surprise come summer. Because of the tilt of the earth's axis, the sun is above the horizon 24 hours a day. The end of the stick's shadow will actually trace out a circle. So make sure you have plenty of pebbles on hand!

Did You Know?

A gnomon (pronounced NO-mon) is an object, like a stick or a pole, that casts a shadow to keep track of the time.

WORDS TO KNOW

arc: a section of a curve or part of a circle.

Northern Hemisphere: the half of the earth north of the equator.

Southern Hemisphere: the half of the earth south of the equator.

equator: the imaginary line around the middle of the earth halfway between the North and South Poles.

Summer sun

Winter sun

Stick

South

Summer shadow

North

Winter shadow

Spring and fall shadow

Chapter 2

HERE COME THE HOURS

Calendars are a good starting point for tracking time. The sun comes up, the sun goes down, the sun comes up again, and on and on for millions of years. As day follows day, we group them into the weeks, months, and years of a calendar. This allows us to easily compare one length of time with another.

A day clearly has two periods: daytime, when the sun is above the horizon, and nighttime, when it's not. But how did we get from day and night to 24 hours? And from there to an hour of 60 minutes, each of which contains 60 seconds? As with the creation of calendars, we have to give credit to the ancient Egyptians.

constellation: a group of stars visible in the night sky that form a pattern.

As you might remember from the first chapter, the Egyptians created a 365-day calendar after noticing that once every 365 days, the star Sothis rose in the sky just before the sun did. Having only one star to set your watch by is hardly enough though, so the Egyptians identified 35 other stars and **constellations** that rose during daylight just like Sothis. The rising of these stars started each of their 10-day-long weeks. By watching these stars, Egyptians were able to keep their calendar on track.

Timekeeping

In addition to rising in daylight, these stars are visible at They rose over the horizon at regular intervals as the earth Observing the way these stars appeared to across the night sky, the Egyptians divided the night into 12 equal parts. Since night and day last about the same length of time, Egyptians decided to divide daytime into 12 parts, too. And that is how the 24-hour day was born.

WORDS TO KNOW

shadow clock: a clock developed by ancient Egyptians that used the sun's shadow to track time.

archaeologist: a scientist who studies ancient people and their cultures by finding and examining things like graves, ruins, tools, and pottery.

Babylonian: someone who lived in Babylon, an ancient city in what is Iraq today.

To track the 12 daytime hours, Egyptians used a **shadow clock**, which is also known as a time stick. Shadow clocks are one of the oldest ways to measure time by the movement of the sun. **Archaeologists** have found shadow clocks dating back more than 3,500 years, but simple ones were probably used even earlier.

A stick stuck in the ground was probably the first shadow clock.

MAKING MINUTES

Like the Egyptians, the **Babylonians** used the movement of the stars to divide both day and night into 12 equal parts. But the Babylonians, who had already made great advances in arithmetic, went even further. They divided each hour into 60 pieces (minutes), and each of those pieces into 60 even smaller parts (seconds).

Why 60? It's hard to say. Most people today count by groups of 10. For example, the number 58 is made up of eight single units and five groups of ten. Mathematicians call this type of number system a **base 10 counting system**. The Babylonians counted by tens, but they also had counting systems based on 2, 4, 12, 24, and—you guessed it—60.

In a **base 60 counting system**, the units column goes from 0 to 59 and then rolls over to 0 as the sixties column changes from 0 to 1. This is what happens on a **digital** clock when you see the minutes reach 59 and then after another minute, the time changes to the next hour.

WORDS TO KNOW

base 10 counting system: a number system based on units of 10.

base 60 counting system: a number system based on units of 60.

digital: presenting data as numbers.

The Years Roll On

The base 60 counting system was in place in the Seleucid Dynasty by the time the leader of the Greek Empire, Alexander the Great, died in 323 BCE. When the generals in his army divided up the empire, General Seleucus became king of the eastern part, which included the city of Babylon. The Seleucids and the Greeks traded with each other, which helped each culture share ideas too. The Greeks adopted the Babylonian timekeeping system and later passed it on to the Romans, who spread it throughout Europe.

In addition to giving us the base 60 counting system, the Seleucid Dynasty may have been the first in the Middle East to keep a continuous record of years as they passed. Before Seleucus took over, these countries tracked years only by referring to who ruled the country at that time. You might say that you were born during the "fifth year of Darius," for example, and everyone who lived in the same area would know what you meant. However, anyone outside the country would be confused and not know how old you were. What if your mother said she was born in the "second year of Ford?" Does this make it easier or harder to know how old she is?

SHADOWS IN YOUR NEIGHBORHOOD

Shadow clocks were a good first attempt at timekeeping, but they aren't very accurate. As you've already learned, the path and length of a gnomon's shadow changes throughout the year, so a time stick used in summer will have different shadows from one used in winter.

The Egyptians were okay with "hours" in the summer lasting longer than "hours" in the winter. Daylight lasted longer in summer than in winter, so for them it was only natural that summer hours be longer. Hours that grow and shrink may have been fine for the Egyptians, but later civilizations wanted an hour to mean the same thing throughout the year.

A *sundial* is a more complex and more accurate version of the shadow clock.

Instead of measuring time by measuring the length of the gnomon's shadow, sundials measure time by tracking which direction the shadow points. The shadow of a sundial's gnomon should point in the same direction at the same time of day throughout the year. But the hour indicated by the gnomon's shadow on a sundial depends on three things: the **angle** of the gnomon, the direction the gnomon faces, and the layout of the hour markers on the face of the sundial.

WORDS TO KNOW

sundial: a tool created by the Greek inventor Anaximander (611–546 BCE) that uses a shadow cast by the sun to determine the time.

angle: the space between two lines that start from the same point, measured in **degrees**.

degree: a unit of measure of a circle. There are 360 degrees in a circle.

A gnomon that rises off the sundial at a steep angle will make a different shadow than one that rises at a shallow angle. If the tip of the gnomon points northeast, it will make different shadows from one pointing north. And, obviously, you can't place the hour markers just anywhere. You need to know enough about the sun's movement that the shadows will fall where they should.

Did You Know?

Noon is the middle of the day, when the sun is at its highest point in the sky. Another word for noon is meridian. When the sun is at its zenith—that is, directly overhead—we can say that the sun is crossing the day's meridian.

To solve these problems, you need to design the sundial and its gnomon based upon your **latitude**. The equator is the line around the middle of the earth that's equally far from the North and South Poles. Latitude is a measure of how far you are north or south of the equator. The Greek astronomer Ptolemy set the equator as 0 degrees latitude, the North Pole as 90 degrees latitude north, and the South Pole as 90 degrees latitude south. All lines of latitude are **parallel** to the equator.

WORDS TO KNOW

latitude: a measure of distance from the equator, in degrees. The North Pole is 90 degrees latitude north and the South Pole is 90 degrees latitude south.

parallel: when two lines going in the same direction can go on forever and never touch, like an "=" sign.

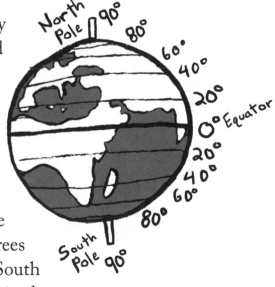

The Problem With a Sundial

While a sundial can tell you the time at your exact location, that time might not match the clock on your wall. Why not? Because the United States, and almost every other country in the world, uses **time zones**.

Within a time zone, the hour and minutes are always the same. The Eastern Time Zone, for example, stretches all the way from Maine to Indiana, so clocks in Portland, Maine, and Indianapolis, Indiana, will always match.

But if you take a walk outside, you'll see that the sun—and sundials—don't work according to time zones. Because of the rotation of the earth, the sun will be directly overhead in Portland long before it's overhead in Indianapolis. This means that a sundial in Portland might say the time is noon and a sundial in Indianapolis might say it's 11:15 in the morning, while the clocks in both towns say it's actually 11:38!

Why 90 degrees? Again, we have the Babylonians to thank.

When the Babylonian calendar considered one year to equal 360 days, they divided circles into 360 sections since years and circles have a lot in common. Just as you would see the same objects again and again if you walked in a circle, the seasons follow each other the same way year after year. Today, we call the sections of a circle "degrees." The North Pole is one-quarter of a circle away from the equator, and one-quarter of 360 degrees is 90 degrees.

WORDS TO KNOW

time zone: a region of the planet, within which the same standard time is used.

For each degree of latitude north or south of the equator, the sun's rays hit the earth at a different angle. On March 21, the spring equinox, the sun is directly over the equator so its rays hit the earth at a 90-degree angle there. This is called a right angle. On that same day in Houston, Texas, at a latitude of about 30 degrees north, the sun shines down at a 60-degree angle. If you live in Anchorage, Alaska, the sun shines at a 30-degree angle, because Anchorage lies at 60 degrees latitude north.

Because the angle of the sun's rays depends on your latitude, a sundial can only be reliable if it is designed for your area.

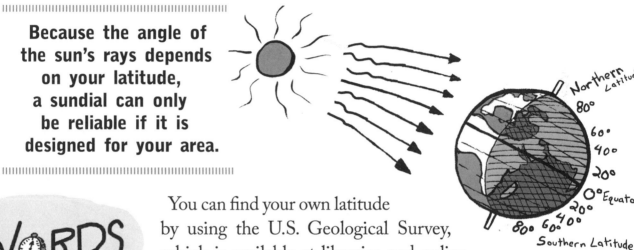

WORDS TO KNOW

sextant: an instrument used to measure the angle between two objects.

quadrant: an instrument used to measure the height of the planets, moon, or stars.

You can find your own latitude by using the U.S. Geological Survey, which is available at libraries and online at geonames.usgs.gov. Click "Search Domestic Names." You can select your state, and then get more specific by typing the name of your town into the "feature name" window.

Another way is to use a **sextant**, a tool that sailors use to help them know where they are on the ocean. You can make your own simple sextant, called a **quadrant**, that will determine your latitude so that you can build an accurate sundial.

MAKE AN EGYPTIAN TIME STICK

Supplies

- piece of wood 20 inches long, 2 inches wide, and 1 inch thick (51 by 5 by 2½ centimeters)
- piece of wood 17 inches long, 2 inches wide, and 1 inch thick (43 by 5 by 2½ centimeters)
- piece of wood 3 inches long, 2 inches wide, and 1 inch thick (7½ by 5 by 2½ centimeters)
- hammer
- several nails
- white paint
- paintbrush
- glass of water or carpenter's level
- pencil
- watch

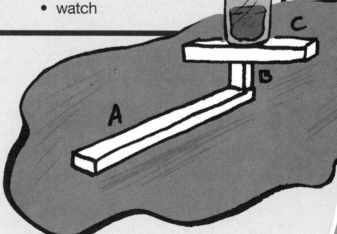

1 To make a time stick, nail the three sections of wood together as shown. Paint the wood white so you'll be able to see shadows on it easily.

2 Before 7:00 in the morning on a sunny day, take the time stick outside and place it on the ground. The back of the top bar should face east—that is, toward the sun. To make sure the time stick is level, fill a glass with water, place it on the stick, and adjust the stick until the water in the glass is level. You could also use a carpenter's level, but learning how to level something the old-fashioned way is a neat trick.

3 At 7 a.m., use the pencil to mark where the shadow of the top bar falls on the stick. Label the mark "7 a.m." The bar is an example of a gnomon, a vertical device that casts a shadow on some sort of ruler or measuring stick to keep track of the time.

4 Go outside each hour from 8 a.m. to 11 a.m., and mark the shadow and time on the stick. At noon, turn the time stick around so that the back of the top bar faces west. When the shadow of the bar reaches the mark you made at 11 a.m., the time will be 1 p.m. As the day goes on, keep labeling the time at each hour until 5 p.m. The five marks on your shadow clock divide the day into six hours before noon and six hours after. So now you can track time like an Egyptian!

rising Sun

7:00 AM

ACTIVITY

MAKE YOUR OWN QUADRANT

Use this quadrant made from a protractor to find your latitude. A protractor is a tool that helps you draw angles on paper.

Supplies

- tape
- clear straw
- protractor
- 1 foot of string (30 centimeters)
- jumbo paper clip or other small object

1 Tape the straw to the protractor so that the straw lies across the center mark and the 90-degree mark.

2 Tie the string to the paper clip, then tape the string to the center mark of the protractor. If you hold the protractor straight up and down with the straw parallel to the ground, the string should pass through the 0-degree mark.

3 To use the quadrant, hold it so that the rounded part of the protractor faces toward you. Look through the straw at an object, such as the top of a building or a tree, and hold the protractor steady. When the string stops swinging, hold it against the protractor and see where it falls on the scale between 0 and 90 degrees. If, for example, the string lies on 37, then you know that the top of the building is at a 37-degree angle from the ground where you are standing.

4 To find your latitude, go outside at night and locate the Big Dipper overhead. Use the pointer stars on the cup of the Big Dipper to find Polaris. Polaris is also known as the North Star because it lies directly over the North Pole. Look through your quadrant at Polaris and find the angle of Polaris over the horizon. This number equals your latitude!

Polaris

ACTIVITY

BUILD YOUR OWN SUNDIAL

Once you have found your latitude, you can create a sundial perfect for your location.

Supplies

- thick white paper
- ruler
- pencil
- protractor (without the straw taped to it)
- scissors
- eraser
- tape or glue
- compass
- glass of water or level

1 At the bottom of the paper, draw line AB. Mark the center of line AB with the point O. This is the 6 o'clock line. At a right angle (90 degrees) to line AB, draw line CO. This is the 12 o'clock line.

2 Use the protractor to draw line OD. The angle COD must be equal in degrees to your latitude. Place the protractor with the O-degree mark on line CO and the 90-degree mark on line AB. If your latitude is, for example, 37 degrees, then make a mark at 37 on the protractor. Then use the ruler to draw a straight line from O through this mark.

3 Somewhere along the line OD, mark a point E. Where you place E will determine how large the finished sundial is. If E is 4 inches from O (10 centimeters), then the finished diagram will be roughly 7 inches by 8 inches (18 by 20 centimeters).

4 From point E, draw a line at a right angle from line OD so it hits line CO. Mark the intersection as point F. Draw a long skinny rectangle next to line OF. Trace the triangle FOE and the rectangle onto a separate sheet of thick paper for your gnomon and cut it out. Set the gnomon aside for now.

5 Going back to your sundial drawing, measure the distance from E to F. Now mark point G on the line CO so that the distance between F and G is the same as between E and F.

continues on next page . . .

6 Draw line QR through point F. Make sure it is parallel to line AB. Draw line ST through point G, making it parallel to AB and QR.

7 Using the protractor, draw a semicircle that begins and ends on line ST with point G as its center. The semicircle can be any size as long as it doesn't go below line QR. Make three marks on the semicircle, 15 degrees apart, to the left and to the right of GF.

8 Using the ruler, draw straight lines from point G through each of these six marks to line QR. You now have seven points on line QR, including point F. Label these points from left to right with the hours 9, 10, 11, 12, 1, 2, and 3. Draw straight lines from each of these points to 0. These will be the hour lines on the finished sundial.

9 From point F, draw a line parallel to the line going from point O to 9. Make this line go all the way to line AB. Label the point where the lines intersect point W.

10 Where line FW crosses the 1, 2, and 3 o'clock lines, mark the points K, L, and M.

11 To mark the points N and P on line FW, measure the distance between L and M. The distance between M and N must be the same. Measure this distance with the ruler, then mark point N. The distance between M and P must be the same as the distance between K and M. Measure this distance, then mark point P.

12 Using the ruler, draw two lines parallel to line FO. One line will connect the point labeled 9 with the line AB, and the other line will connect the point labeled 3 with the line AB, meeting point W.

13 Using the ruler, draw lines from point O through points N and P until you hit the line from 3 to point W. These are the 4 and 5 o'clock lines so mark them 4 and 5 on the line from 3 to point W.

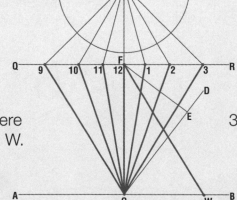

14 On the line from 9 to line AB, mark the points 7 and 8. The distance between 7 and 9 must be the same as the distance between 3 and 5. Similarly, the distance between 8 and 9 must match the distance between 3 and 4. Draw lines from point O to 7 and point O to 8. These lines are the 7 and 8 o'clock lines. Change point W to 6. Where 9 crosses line AB, also mark point 6.

15 You can now erase all the lines other than the hour lines. Or you can place another sheet of paper on top of this one and trace only the hour lines onto this new sheet.

16 Make a slot along the 12 o'clock line on your sundial for the skinny rectangle on your gnomon to fit inside. This way the gnomon can stand upright. Place the gnomon so that point F on the gnomon lies at point O on the sundial, then tape or glue the pieces together.

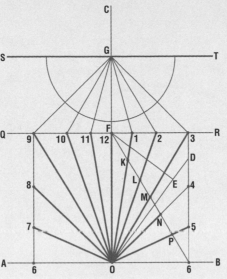

You can glue the sundial to wood or cardboard to make it sturdier. Then place it outside with the 12 o'clock line pointing exactly north. Use a compass to find north, or wait until noon and position the sundial so that the gnomon doesn't create a shadow. Use a glass of water or a carpenter's level to make sure the sundial is level.

If you've positioned everything correctly, the gnomon will point directly at Polaris!

Note: This sundial would be upside-down for anyone living in the Southern Hemisphere. To fix this, reverse the order of the hour markers so that the digits across the line QR read "3, 2, 1, 12, 11, 10, 9." Switch points 7 and 8 with points 5 and 4.

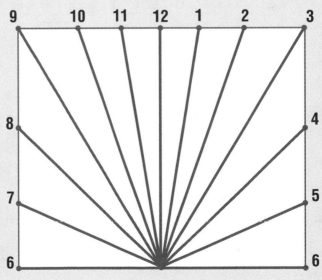

Chapter 3

TELLING TIME AFTER TWILIGHT

Shadow clocks and sundials are extremely useful timekeeping devices. But can you use them to tell time on cloudy days or during the night or in the middle of a thunderstorm or during a sandstorm?

Okay, so maybe timekeeping devices that rely on the sun aren't always the best idea. The ancient Egyptians realized this, so when the sun wasn't visible overhead, they used a more down-to-earth substance to track time: water.

The *clepsydra*, from the Greek words for "water thief," is a clock made from water and a bucket.

Sound confusing? Imagine a container with a small hole in the bottom that is plugged with clay. If the container is filled with water to a mark on the inside and a tiny hole is poked in the clay, the water will start dripping out. It would be easy for you to use a watch to track the hours, marking the water level in the container as each hour passes. This is a simple clepsydra. The clepsydra measures hours only from when the water starts flowing, which can be at any time during the day. But once the container is empty, you'll know how many hours you can track using this clepsydra.

SUNNY DAYS MAKE TIME PASS FASTER

Because water generally flows at a steady rate, an hour measured with a clepsydra will be about the same throughout the year. But Egyptian hours weren't the same length throughout the year. When daylight lasted longer in the summer, the hours were longer as well. To make clepsydras match their hours, Egyptians used a different set of marks for each month of the year.

Timekeeping

Many different cultures used clepsydras until the 1700s. As the years passed, Greek and Roman **horologists** created more complicated designs for clepsydras, such as air-filled containers that sank into the water as the hours passed. Water flows a bit faster from a full bucket than from a nearly empty one because of the weight of the water itself. Horologists tried to control the pressure of the water so that it flowed at a **precise** rate all the time.

horologist: a person who makes clocks and measures time.

precise: exact or detailed.

astronomer: a person who studies the stars and planets.

reservoir: a large tank or lake used to store water.

mechanical: done automatically or as if by machine, not by a person.

mechanism: a machine or part of a machine.

Later, clepsydras had devices that floated on the surface of the water and identified the hours by either pointing a rotating hand or ringing gongs or bells.

One of the largest examples of a water clock is the Tower of the Winds, which still stands in Athens, Greece. A man named Andronicus, who was an **astronomer** from Macedonia, designed the tower sometime between 200 and 50 BCE. Known at the time as the Horologion, the tower is 42 feet tall (13 meters) and 26 feet in diameter (8 meters). It is shaped like an octagon, with the walls facing toward the eight main points on a compass: north, northeast, east, southeast, and so on.

The water for the clepsydra flowed down from a **reservoir** on the south side of the roof. Little of the clepsydra survives today, but it seems to have had a **mechanical** device that displayed the hours on the outside of the tower.

The Chinese began using water clocks at about the same time as the Egyptians.

Did You Know?

The original Tower of the Winds had a bronze figure that pointed in the direction of the wind. The tower had two timekeeping systems: a 24-hour clepsydra and a set of eight sundials. A sundial hung on each of the eight walls, underneath a sculpture of the figure that represented the wind that blew in that direction.

Between 700 and 1000 CE the Chinese created clepsydras that used waterwheels. Water would flow into a small bucket attached to a wheel until the bucket was so heavy that the wheel turned. A new bucket would then be filled, turning the wheel again. As the wheel rotated, it moved **mechanisms** that displayed the time and different astronomical events.

The Niagara Falls of water clocks must surely be one created by Su Sung in China around 1090 CE. The emperor of China ordered Su Sung to create the greatest clock in history.

Building the water clock took Su Sung's team of men at least eight years: two to build a working wooden model, two to cast the bronze parts of the clock, and four more to finish everything else.

Su Sung

It was the most amazing clock the world had ever seen, standing over 30 feet tall (9 meters).

mannequin: a model of a person.

The clock had an automatically rotating globe of the heavens and moving **mannequins** that rang bells and displayed tablets indicating the hours of the day. When China was invaded in 1126, though, the clock was stolen. Nothing remains of it today.

Luckily, Su Sung wrote and illustrated a book about his clock, and different copies of the book were discovered centuries later. Because of his book, the modern world knows about this great achievement of the past.

SEEING TOMORROW'S STARS TODAY

A much more complicated nighttime clock—one that dates back to at least 400 CE—is the **astrolabe**. The astrolabe was based on the ancient Greek view of the **universe**, which had Earth at the center with the stars circling around.

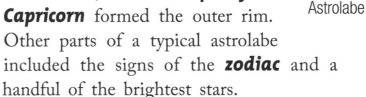

On an astrolabe, the stars and planets were drawn flat on a metal disk to make a visible map of the sky. Polaris, which seems not to move, was placed at the center of the astrolabe, and the **Tropic of Capricorn** formed the outer rim. Other parts of a typical astrolabe included the signs of the **zodiac** and a handful of the brightest stars.

Astrolabe

By inserting a metal plate designed for a specific latitude onto the astrolabe, someone using it could determine the time of day or night. It was possible to calculate when sunrise and sunset would happen, or find the rising or setting time of any star. It was even possible to figure out exactly how the night sky would look at any point in the past or future!

astrolabe: a device that measures the **altitude** of the sun or a star to determine latitude and time.

altitude: how high something is above sea level.

universe: everything that exists, everywhere.

Tropic of Capricorn: the line of latitude 23 degrees south of the equator.

zodiac: a band of stars that includes all the planets and is divided into 12 named constellations.

navigate: to find a route to another place.

|||||||||||||||||||||||||||||||||||||||||||||||||||||||||||||||||||||||||||||||||

Sailors used astrolabes to *navigate* until the eighteenth century, when it was replaced by the sextant.

|||||||||||||||||||||||||||||||||||||||||||||||||||||||||||||||||||||||||||||||||

A Timekeeper by Any Other Name

Whether you call it a sandglass or an hourglass, one thing is true about this shapely timekeeping device—you're probably calling it something that it's not.

While some sandglasses hold an amount of sand that takes 60 minutes to flow from the top chamber to the bottom, many do not. Sandglasses were often designed for a specific purpose, such as measuring the time it took to cook bread or to give a speech. These sandglasses held only as much material as was needed for their purpose. What's more, these timers usually held powdered eggshell or marble dust—no sand at all!

The hourglass doesn't show up in history until about 700 years ago in Italy, when mechanical clocks were already being invented. They were especially useful on ships, because the rocking motion made sundials or water clocks useless. Sailors generally used a half-hour-long sandglass to measure the four-hour period they stood watch on deck. At the end of each half hour, the sailor on watch flipped the sandglass and rang a bell to let others know the time, ringing the bell once after the first half hour, twice after the second half hour, and so on. At eight bells a new sailor would take over watch.

THE GLASS IS TURNED, SOUND FOUR BELLS MR. SQUIB.

FLIP

AYE, SIR!

ACTIVITY

MAKE YOUR OWN SANDGLASS

You don't need to be a glass blower to make your own sandglass.

Supplies

- 2 identical plastic bottles
- sand
- sifter or cheesecloth
- scissors
- piece of cardboard
- needle
- tape
- permanent marker

1 Make sure that the sand and bottles are perfectly dry. Any moisture will make the sand clump. Leave the materials outside on a sunny day to dry.

2 Sift the sand through a sifter or cheesecloth so that all the particles are about the same size. Large particles or a piece of shell can stop your sandglass from working.

3 Cut the cardboard into a circle that has the same diameter as the neck of the bottles. Make a small hole in the center of the cardboard with the needle.

TAPE

4 Fill one bottle half full of sand. Tape the bottle necks together with the piece of cardboard in between. Turn the bottles over, and time how long the sand takes to flow from top to bottom. Adjust the amount of sand in the bottle or the size of the hole in the cardboard so that your sandglass (or in this case "sandplastic") measures out an even amount of time. It might take a few tries to get it right. Write this number on the bottles so you don't forget it! Once you're finished, tape the necks securely and put your timer to use. You can make different timers for different activities.

ACTIVITY

WATCH THE HOURS FLOW BY

You can make a simple clepsydra of your own, but instead of marking the container that water flows out of, you'll mark the container that water flows into.

Supplies

- large coffee can
- acrylic paint
- paintbrush
- hammer
- needle
- electrical or duct tape
- 2 pieces of wood 9½ inches long and 4½ inches wide (24 centimeters long and 11½ centimeters wide)
- 3 pieces of wood 5 inches long and 1½ inches wide (12½ centimeters long and 4 centimeters wide)
- nails
- quart-sized glass jar

1 Paint the coffee can with acrylic paint inside and out to help keep it from rusting. Use the hammer and needle to poke a very small hole in the bottom of the can. If the hole turns out to be too large, cover it with electrical tape or duct tape and poke another smaller hole.

2 Stand up the large pieces of wood and nail two of the small pieces flat across the top to create a stand for the coffee can. Make sure to leave a gap between them. Nail the third small piece of wood across the back of the stand. Place the glass jar underneath the stand.

3 Hold your finger over the hole in the coffee can while you fill it with water. Then place the can on the stand so that the water drains into the glass jar.

36

4 As each hour passes, mark the current level of the water in the glass jar—not the can—until the can is empty.

5 Your simple timer is easy to use. If you have to do two hours of homework before you can go outside and play soccer, fill the glass jar with water to the two-hour mark. Hold your finger over the hole in the can, pour the water in, and let it flow. When the water stops dripping, and the water level in your jar is at 2 hours, you can hit the playing field!

A Water Alarm Clock

With a little extra work—and very understanding parents—you could even turn your clepsydra into an alarm clock. Let's say, for example, that your bedtime is 9 p.m. and you have to wake up at 6 a.m. to get ready for school. You want to set up the flow of water so that the jar overflows after exactly nine hours, the amount you sleep at night. At bedtime, fill the can with more water than the jar will hold. Position the clepsydra on a shelf over your head. Come 6:00 in the morning, the water will flow over the top of the jar and start dripping on your head.

FINDING TIME IN THE STARS

Just like sailors in the sixteenth and seventeenth centuries, you can use a device called a nocturnal to tell time by the stars at night. The nocturnal was developed in the thirteenth century. Astronomers already knew that while most stars moved through the sky at night, Polaris stayed in place. Polaris lies directly over the North Pole, so as the earth spins on its axis, the position of Polaris in the sky doesn't change.

A nocturnal is a device to take advantage of the reliability of Polaris and the location of other stars around it. Since you must be able to see Polaris, you can use a nocturnal only if you live in the Northern Hemisphere. Even into the seventeenth century, sailors spent most of their time north of the equator, so no device similar to the nocturnal was ever created for the Southern Hemisphere. Most nocturnals were made of wood or metal because they were used aboard a ship. You can use almost any sturdy material.

Supplies

- coffee can or bowl, at least 4 inches in diameter (10 centimeters)
- pen
- protractor
- 8½-by-11-inch piece of poster board or cardboard (2½ by 28 centimeters)
- scissors
- hole punch
- threaded ½-inch-long piece of pipe (1¼ centimeters)
- 2 metal nuts open at both ends to fit on the pipe

1 Use the coffee can or bowl to draw a circle in the middle of the poster board or cardboard. Use the protractor to divide the circle into 12 sections, with each section measuring 30 degrees. Write "January" in one section. Then go counterclockwise around the circle writing the names of the other 11 months.

2 Draw three small lines in each section, every 7½ degrees, so that each section is divided into four smaller sections. These four smaller pieces are the weeks within each month, with the first week on the right and the last week on the left.

3 Mark the center of the circle with a dot. Draw a straight handle roughly 5 inches long and 1 inch wide coming out from the June/July sections (12½ by 2½ centimeters). Cut out the circle and its handle as one piece.

4 On the poster board, draw another circle that's 1 inch smaller in diameter than your first circle (2½ centimeters smaller). Use the protractor to divide this circle into 24 equal sections, with each section measuring 15 degrees. Label one section "12M" for midnight, and go counterclockwise labeling the other hours, starting with 1 a.m. Draw three small lines in each hour section so that each hour is divided into four equal quarter hours.

5 Before you cut out this circle, you are going to draw three "teeth" on the outside of it. This part must be done carefully to make sure your nocturnal can do its job. The teeth will have one straight edge and one curved edge as shown in the illustration. Each will be labeled with the name of a constellation.

6 Draw the straight edge for the first tooth at exactly 63.4 degrees counterclockwise from midnight. This edge should line up with 4:14 a.m. on the circle. Label this tooth "BD" for the Big Dipper.

7 Draw the straight edge for the second tooth at 124.4 degrees counterclockwise from midnight. This edge should line up with 8:18 a.m. Label this tooth "LD" for the Little Dipper.

8 Draw the straight edge for the third tooth at 94.7 degrees clockwise from midnight. This edge should line up with 5:41 p.m. Label this tooth "C" for Cassiopeia.

continues on next page . . .

9 Draw the curved edges for all three teeth. Mark the center of the circle with a dot. Cut out this circle and the teeth, leaving the teeth attached to the circle.

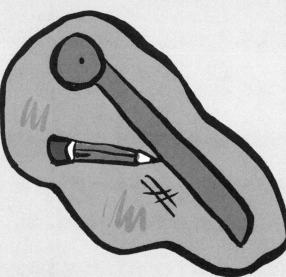

10 Draw a third circle on the poster board, this one just over 1 inch in diameter (2½ centimeters). Mark the center of the circle with a dot. From the dot, draw a line that's at least 9 inches long (23 centimeters). Make sure this line is at least 4 inches longer than the diameter of your largest circle (10 centimeters). Draw another line parallel to this one that connects just at the edge of the circle. Cut out this circle and its pointer arm.

11 Through the center of each circle, punch a hole that is just large enough for the pipe. Place the circles on the pipe, with the smallest circle on top of the middle one, which is on top of the largest one.

12 Screw the nuts onto the pipe. The circles should be loose enough that you can move them, but not so loose that they can move on their own.

13 To use the nocturnal, choose the Big Dipper, the Little Dipper, or Cassiopeia. Here we'll use the Big Dipper since we used this constellation in chapter two to find Polaris. Set the tooth marked "BD" on the correct date. If the date is May 7, for example, the straight edge of the tooth should line up with the rightmost mark in May.

14 Hold the nocturnal at arm's length with the handle pointing down. Use the pointer stars on the Big Dipper to find Polaris, then move the nocturnal so that you can see Polaris through the pipe in the center of your nocturnal. While keeping Polaris in sight through the pipe, move the pointer arm until the long edge lines up with the pointer stars in the Big Dipper. The edge of the pointer across the hour sections will show what time it is, to within about 15 minutes!

NOTE: If you want to use the Little Dipper to measure time, set the date with the "LD" tooth on the date, spot Polaris through the nocturnal as usual, and line up the pointer arm with Kochab, the star in the upper right corner of the Little Dipper's cup. To use Cassiopeia as a guide, use the "C" tooth to mark the date and line up the pointer arm with Schedar. Look at the picture if you're not sure where these two stars are located.

Chapter 4

WHAT IS
A CLOCK, ANYWAY?

What do you picture when you think of a clock? A round surface with arms that point at numbers from 1 to 12? A small box that displays red numbers and flashes 12:00 whenever you lose electricity? These are both examples of clocks. Their differences show that clocks come in all sorts of shapes, sizes, and designs.

> **To be a clock, a device requires two things: a constant or repetitive process that marks off equal pieces of time and a way to track the pieces and display the results.**

An Egyptian shadow clock meets both of these requirements. The movement of the shadow across the board marks off the hours of the day, and this same board displays the result of that movement. The clepsydra and sundial work similarly. The sun itself is a clock. This is true because it moves steadily across the sky, and, if you know what you're doing, you can tell time by measuring its location overhead.

TIMEKEEPING METHODS

Different cultures have created many types of clocks over the past 10,000 years. While they didn't work as accurately as today's clocks and watches, they were good enough for their time.

Oil Lamp Clock: Just as a water clock measures the flow of water, an oil clock measures the level of oil in a lamp. As the wick burns in an oil lamp, the level of oil remaining in the lamp steadily drops. You can track time by comparing oil levels against marks on the glass reservoir that holds the oil.

Incense Clock: Most people burn **incense** sticks and cones because they like the smell, but incense can also help you track time.

incense: a slow-burning wood that produces a pleasant smell when burned.

T|mekeeping

If, for example, an incense stick takes one-and-a-half hours to burn all the way down, then you can use the same kind of incense stick to measure this length of time whenever you need to.

The Chinese came up with the idea of using incense for timekeeping. Incense makers made their sticks a certain length and width so they all burned the same amount of time.

As with most inventions, many variations on the incense clock have been used over the years.

Some Chinese incense makers added several perfumes to their incense so that the aroma would change as the stick burned. If you started smelling, say, jasmine, you would know that 30 minutes had passed, then once the air filled with a musky smell, you would know it was an hour later.

One example of a fancy incense alarm clock comes from the nineteenth century. The "clock" is a long piece of wood carved to look like a boat, with a dragon's head at the front. Inside the boat, a piece of pewter holds the incense so that the wood doesn't burn.

A person using this clock places an incense stick flat on the piece of pewter, then lays thin strings at intervals over the incense. Each of the strings has a small metal ball tied to each end. As the incense burns, it also burns through the strings, which causes the metal balls to fall into a bowl placed below the clock. The noise of the metal hitting the bowl sounds like the chime of a modern clock. As long as the strings are placed evenly across the incense, the clock will be fairly reliable.

Selling by the Candle

The seventeenth-century poet John Milton described a way to use candles for timekeeping called "selling by the candle." During an auction, the auctioneer pushed a pin into the side of a burning candle. People could bid for an item until the candle burned down and the pin fell out. When this happened, the bidding stopped and the person with the high bid at that moment won the auction to buy the item.

Rolling Ball Clock: Have you ever seen a clock in a gift shop that uses metal balls to display the hours and minutes? The machine usually has a motorized arm that lifts a ball onto a series of ramps, and the ball rolls until it lands in a slot for minutes. When the minutes slot fills up, one ball falls into a space for hours, and the rest roll to the bottom.

While fun to watch, these rolling ball clocks aren't very interesting as a timekeeping innovation because what keeps the time is the motor that drives the arm, not the metal balls themselves.

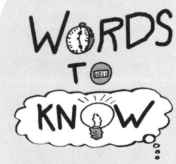

gear: a toothed wheel or cylinder that connects with another toothed part to send motion from one rotating body to another.

The metal balls just display the results.

William Congreve

A better example of a rolling ball clock was invented in 1808 by Sir William Congreve (1772–1828). The clock is made of a series of interlocking *gears* and a metal table that tilts back and forth like a seesaw.

Timekeeping

A metal ball runs down a zigzag path cut into this metal table. After 30 seconds it reaches the end of the path where it hits a catch that tilts the table in the other direction. The tilting of the table helps drive the gears of the clock. Hours and minutes are displayed on dials, and the moving ball indicates seconds as it passes under small bridges on the metal table.

Calculations show that the metal ball travels more than 12,000 miles in a year!

Hand Sundial: Until the eighteenth century, most people could not afford a clock of their own. They measured time by the movement of the sun, bells rung in church towers, and sundials on public buildings. In the eighteenth century, European farmers came up with a cheap way to make a hand sundial with nothing more than their hands and a short stick.

ACTIVITY

MAKE A HAND SUNDIAL

Put time in the palm of your hand! A stick can do a surprisingly good job of telling time.

Supplies

- your hands
- sunny day
- stick or pen about 6 inches long (15 centimeters)

1 If you're measuring time in the morning, face the west, away from the horizon where the sun rose.

2 With your left hand palm up, place the stick close to the base of your left thumb at an angle toward the opposite side of your hand. Make the angle formed by the stick and your palm roughly equal to your latitude. (Check out the activities in chapter two if you need to find your latitude.)

3 The shadow of the stick across your hand will give you a general idea of the time.

4 To measure time after noon, hold the stick at the base of your right thumb and hold your hand, palm up, facing east. Your pointer finger marks 7 p.m., your middle finger 6 p.m., your ring finger 5 p.m., and so on. The hours go down from there.

Latitudes for some cities:

- New York, New York: 40°34'N
- Chicago, Illinois: 41°51'N
- Miami, Florida: 25°46'N
- San Francisco, California: 37°46'N
- Los Angeles, California: 34°03'N
- Houston, Texas: 29°45'N
- Johannesburg, South Africa: 26°11'S
- Montreal, Canada: 46°48'N
- Sydney, Australia: 33°52'S
- Hong Kong, China: 22°18'N

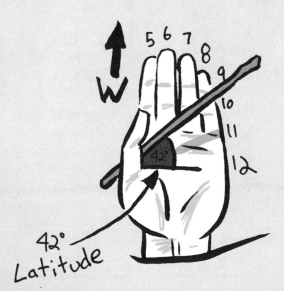

ACTIVITY

MAKE YOUR OWN CANDLE CLOCK

It's easy to make a clock using a candle, but you need to use a certain kind of candle. It must be the same width from top to bottom, not tapered at the top. And it must be less than 1½ inches in diameter so that the burning wax falls down the outside of the candle (4 centimeters). Caution: This activity uses matches and an open flame, so ask an adult to supervise.

Supplies

- straight candle less than 1½ inches in diameter (4 centimeters)
- candleholder
- matches
- marker

1 Place the candle in the candleholder, then measure the length of the candle that is visible.

2 Light the candle and let it burn for either 30 minutes or an hour. Make sure to keep the candle away from open windows and any other drafts because a breeze will make the candle melt faster.

3 Blow out the candle. Once the wax has cooled, measure the candle again to see how much of it has melted away. If, for example, the candle burned three-quarters of an inch in one hour, then make a mark from the top of the candle every three-quarters of an inch (2 centimeters). Number the marks.

4 Now all you need to do to track that amount of time is light your candle. The melting wax will mark the passage of time.

ACTIVITY

MAKE YOUR OWN INCENSE CLOCK

Here's a way to tell time and make your house smell good, too. By placing weighted strings at equal distances along a burning incense stick, you can keep track of time as the incense burns. Caution: This activity uses incense and matches, so ask an adult to supervise.

Supplies

- foil loaf pan
- gravel
- metal cookie sheet
- incense stick
- ruler
- pen
- thread
- scissors
- 12 small metal weights or washers
- matches

1 Fill the loaf pan almost to the top with gravel. Place the loaf pan on the cookie sheet.

2 Using a ruler, measure six equal distances along the length of the incense stick. Mark these with a pen. Lay the incense stick down the middle of the loaf pan.

3 Cut six pieces of thread. Tie a washer to each end of each piece of thread. Lay the strings across the stick at pen marks. The washers should hang over either side of the pan, but not touch the cookie sheet.

4 Light the incense stick and let it burn for about 30 seconds, then blow it out and let it smolder. Start the stopwatch and time how long it takes until the first string burns through. The washers will drop onto the metal baking sheet and make a ringing noise to alert you. Once you know how long each burning interval takes, you can use incense to keep track of time.

Chapter 5

ESCAPING THE TIME TRAPS OF OLD

By the year 1000 CE, European and Asian civilizations had several timekeeping systems to choose from, but still none was very accurate. Sundials gave only a rough idea of the time. Hot weather **evaporated** water in a clepsydra, and in cold weather the water could freeze. Candles, oil, and incense all gave a general idea of the time, but they were far from precise.

WORDS TO KNOW

evaporate: when a liquid heats up and changes to a gas.

manufacture: to make something by machine, in a large factory.

This was fine, because most people didn't need to know exactly what time it was. Farmers worked from sunrise to sunset, and they hardly needed a clock to tell them when the sun was up.

As **manufacturing** grew, so did cities. More and more Europeans left the farms to work in factories that made clothing, glassware, and iron tools. Today we use clocks and computer systems to track an employee's work hours, but in the factories of the 1200s you had to show up for work "when it was light enough to make out a person's face" at a certain distance. Can you imagine how many arguments this must have caused?

The Roman Catholic Church, which had a lot of influence throughout Europe at this time, also used general descriptions for when events should occur. Prayers were "in late morning" and "just before sunset." Monks had to say prayers in a particular order, however, and if they started too late, their schedule would be off for the rest of the day.

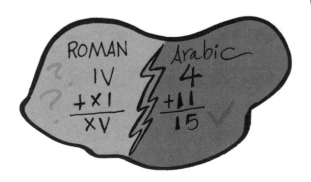

ROMAN

$$\begin{array}{r} IV \\ + XI \\ \hline XV \end{array}$$

Arabic

$$\begin{array}{r} 4 \\ + 11 \\ \hline 15 \end{array}$$

Did You Know?
The relaxed attitude toward time started changing in the 1300s when Arabic numerals (1, 2, 3, 4, 5 . . .) largely replaced Roman numerals (I, II, III, IV, V . . .) in Europe. This system made adding, subtracting, multiplying, and dividing much easier, which helped manufacturers to be more precise and productive.

Timekeeping

Most Europeans still used the system of uneven hours that the Egyptians had invented thousands of years earlier. This meant that work and prayer times shifted throughout the year as the length of daylight grew and shrank. But busier schedules were more difficult to manage. Europeans needed a more accurate timekeeping system. Little did they know, Asian horologists had already found the basis for something better.

TALES OF TICK-TOCK

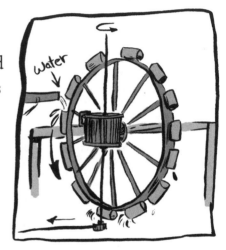

In Su Sung's fabulous water clock, water flowed into a bucket until the weight of the bucket was so heavy that it tripped a lever on the clock. The clock turned until the bucket was past the lever. Then the lever snapped back into place to stop the wheel from turning until the next bucket filled. It took only 24 seconds to fill a bucket and rotate the 30-foot-tall waterwheel (9 meters).

escapement: a device that regulates short periods of time so they are always the same length.

To keep time accurately, a clock must divide and measure time in small, regular chunks over and over again.

Do you have a clock that goes tick-tock? The movement of the **escapement** is what creates the familiar tick-tock sound that people associate with old-fashioned clocks. That regular beat means the clock is tracking equal intervals of time. Clocks rely on movement that is regularly timed and evenly measured. Escapements make this possible.

Escapement Escapades

The principle behind escapements is simple: stop something from moving right now so that when it does move again, it will move with more force. Imagine Su Sung's water clock without an escapement. Water flows into a bucket, but before the bucket fills up, the wheel starts turning. It turns quickly at first, but then slows a little and finally stops. Maybe a new bucket lands right under the water, but maybe not.

The lever on Su Sung's clock is an example of an escapement. As long as the water kept flowing, the clock would rotate exactly 10 degrees every 24 seconds, turning the main shaft of the waterwheel and driving other gears that moved the time-telling displays on the rest of the clock.

EUROPEAN ESCAPE

The idea for a more mechanical escapement first appears in the mid-1200s in the sketchbooks of a French architect named Villard de Honnecourt. He drew a wheel with spokes, several axles, a weight,

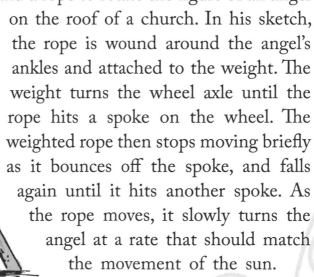

and a rope to rotate the figure of an angel on the roof of a church. In his sketch, the rope is wound around the angel's ankles and attached to the weight. The weight turns the wheel axle until the rope hits a spoke on the wheel. The weighted rope then stops moving briefly as it bounces off the spoke, and falls again until it hits another spoke. As the rope moves, it slowly turns the angel at a rate that should match the movement of the sun.

Honnecourt never built his clock. But mechanical clocks using a similar design started appearing in the late 1200s and early 1300s.

Instead of a rope, these clocks used a **verge escapement (crown wheel)**. This escapement consists of a vertical metal rod (the verge) with two paddles, called pallets, and a spoked wheel. When the wheel turns, a spoke hits one pallet and turns the verge to knock the pallet out of the way. As the verge turns, the other pallet hits the spoked wheel, and gets knocked out of the way. This turns the verge back in the other direction where the first pallet hits the wheel again. The spoked wheel wants to spin quickly because of the weight on it, but the pallets let it turn only one spoke at a time.

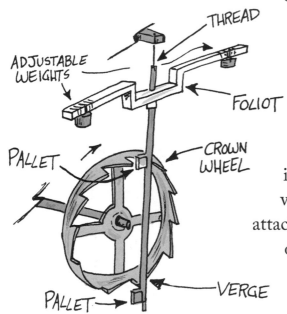

THREAD

ADJUSTABLE WEIGHTS

FOLIOT

PALLET

CROWN WHEEL

PALLET

VERGE

The speed at which the wheel turns is determined by the **foliot**. This is a bar with weights on the end of each arm that's attached to the verge. By moving the weights on the arms, you can make the escapement move faster or slower. You've probably noticed a similar effect on a teeter-totter. If you sit close to the end of a teeter-totter, you can lift more weight than if you sit near the middle. Similarly, if the weight is moved to the end of a foliot, the escapement will move more slowly because it's harder to move the weight.

THE POWER OF GEARS

Long before the 1300s, Europeans were using gears in windmills and watermills. By arranging the gears the right way, mill operators could increase the power of wind and water to move millstones that weighed several tons. They used millstones to grind grain.

Have you ridden a bicycle with multiple gears? Then you know what gears can do. When you ride up a hill, you switch your gears to make pedaling easier. When you ride down a hill, you change to a higher gear to get the most power with only a little bit of pedaling. Using these same ideas, the first clockmakers combined gears with verge escapements to transfer the small back-and-forth motion of the paddled rod into more power.

What did they do with this power? They automated clock functions that people were doing by hand. Monks had always monitored clepsydras, candle clocks, or hourglasses, then rung bells to mark the hours and the times for prayer.

Thanks to the regular ticking of the escapement and the use of many gears, clocks could now automatically ring bells each hour.

BONG!

Ringing bells was the only thing the first mechanical clocks did. They had no faces or moving arms, only gears and levers made to strike a bell. At first these clocks struck a bell only once each hour. Striking a bell a number of times equal to the hour came in the mid-1300s, when clockmakers figured out how to use a separate set of gears to count off the hours.

These early mechanical clocks were expensive, huge, and heavy. Most were placed in churches, cathedrals, and government buildings because the weighted rope that moved the escapement was really long and needed to drop a long distance. Towers and church steeples were the only buildings tall enough. The clock at Wells Cathedral in England was 4 feet high (1.2 meters). Try fitting that on your nightstand!

BUT ARE THEY BETTER?

Mechanical clocks lost or gained up to 15 minutes a day and people had to look at sundials to reset them. The escapement was an important innovation, but early clockmakers struggled to make gears work smoothly. The teeth on the gears stuck together or were too loose. Oiling the gears made them turn better, but then the oil collected dirt and dust that slowed the machine. The temperature of the air made the oil thicker in the summer and thinner in the winter, which also affected the clock's gears. Churches needed someone to clean and oil the gears and reset the hour hand every day.

Getting Creative

Just as Su Sung and other horologists had included moving astronomical displays in their clepsydra, the builders of the first mechanical clocks soon added many moving parts to their creations. An Italian named Giovanni de Dondi spent 16 years in the middle of the 1300s building a 24-hour clock that included the movement of the planets and the moon. The clock in the Wells Cathedral, built around 1392, still exists today. It has figures of knights that joust every hour.

But in other ways, mechanical clocks of fourteenth-century Europe were an improvement. The clocks worked day and night, summer and winter, and they didn't need a person to watch the water flow and then ring a bell to let everyone else know an hour had passed. When hour hands were invented, people could look at the church tower to know the time instead of counting how many times the bell had rung.

With the introduction of the escapement, the idea that hours should be longer in the summer and shorter in the winter faded away. Yes, people could move the weights on the foliot to adjust how quickly time passed, but it was easier to adjust to the idea that hours should be the same length throughout the year.

Did You Know? In the earliest mechanical clock designs, the hour hand didn't move. Instead, the face labeled with the hours was another gear that turned as time passed.

Mechanical clocks had begun to change the way people lived their lives.

Having clocks visible on churches and city halls also got rid of the messy way that employees and employers tracked work hours. Instead of starting work "when it was light enough to make out a person's face," people started and stopped work at particular times.

ACTIVITY

- -

EASY ESCAPEMENT

Escapements have improved over the years, from Su Sung's water escapement to the tiny escapement we have in our wristwatches today.

Supplies

- 2 big pieces of tissue paper
- scissors
- 12-inch-long bamboo stick (30½ centimeters)
- clear tape

- straw
- jumbo paperclip
- light string
- penny
- stopwatch

1 Cut the tissue paper into smaller pieces, each 3 inches wide and 12 inches long (7½ by 30½ centimeters).

2 Lay the bamboo stick on a table. Tape one end of each piece of tissue paper on each end of the bamboo. Tape them securely into place.

CUT!

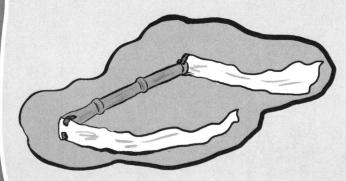

3 Cut the straw so you have a piece about 2 inches long (5 centimeters). Tape it perpendicularly across the middle of your bamboo stick, with most of it hanging down in the same direction as the tissue paper.

4 Uncurl the jumbo paperclip and push it through the straw. Leave about half the paperclip hanging out the lower end, and about ½ inch sticking out the top end (just over 1 centimeter). At the top, bend the paperclip around itself to create a small loop. Thread a piece of string about 6 inches long (15 centimeters) through the loop and tie a knot to secure it to the paperclip.

5 Bend the paperclip on the lower end at a 90-degree angle, and then bend it twice more at 90-degree angles so you create a small square from the paperclip up toward the bamboo. Bend the last side at a slight angle to the right. The paperclip forms the escapement.

6 Tape the string holding the escapement to the middle of a doorway. It needs to hang so that the bamboo stick can spin around without hitting anything.

7 Cut another piece of string about 12 inches long (about 30 centimeters). Tape one end to the bottom part of the straw and wind it around the straw clockwise.

8 Tape the penny to the other end of the string and slip it through the slightly bent square so that it sits on the outside. Once you let go, the penny should be the driving weight that will spin your bamboo stick around at a constant rate.

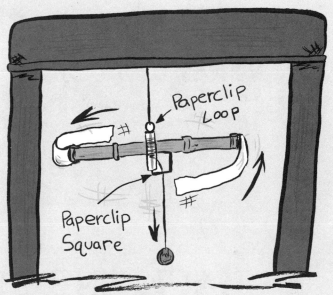

Paperclip LOOP

Paperclip Square

9 Time your air clock escapement. Does it take the same amount of time to rotate each time around? What is controlling the speed of the movement?

Chapter 6

BACK AND FORTH AND BACK AND FORTH

By the year 1400, people were becoming more aware of the value of time in terms of work and play. Clockmakers worked to make clocks more *portable*. They wanted to sell their goods to everyone, and the only way to do this was to make smaller clocks that cost less.

As clockmakers gained skill at shaping metal to small sizes for smaller gears, they created clocks that could be carried while traveling. By 1500, wealthy Europeans were buying small clocks in a frenzy. These clocks were often covered with jewels and gold. Queen Elizabeth I owned a small ring watch that scratched her fingers like an alarm at particular times of day.

Many of the smaller clocks, however, were still designed very much like the earliest mechanical clocks. They still used a long, weighted cord to move the foliot and verge escapement that regulated the gears. In many situations, such as sailing on the ocean or riding in a bouncy horse-drawn carriage, a weight-driven clock was next to worthless.

WORDS TO KNOW

portable: easily moved around.

mainspring: the largest and most important spring in a watch or clock.

SPRINGING A NEW TIME SOLUTION

Between 1500 and 1510, a locksmith named Peter Henlein from the German town of Nuremberg discovered how to drive the gears of a clock with springs. Yes, springs! Do you think of pogo sticks and slinkys? These springs are wound-up coils that look like a spiced curly French fry. But springs come in many shapes. Henlein used springs rolled up in a tight spiral, kind of like a cinnamon bun.

In his spring-driven creation, which Henlein called his Nuremberg Egg, the **mainspring** could slowly unwind to drive the gears.

Peter Henlein

By replacing the heavy weights that drove the escapement, the mainspring made it possible for clockmakers to create smaller clocks and watches—even portable ones. The springs weren't perfect, because as they unwound, the gears of the clock slowed. And if the spring unwound completely, the clock stopped.

To keep a spring-driven clock running properly, its owner had to wind up the spring several times a day.

To solve the problem of the mainspring's uneven power, Jacob Zech of Prague invented the *fusee*, or spiral pulley, around 1525. The fusee is a cone-shaped, grooved pulley that smooths out the power of the mainspring. It turns slowly when the spring has lots of power and gets faster as the spring is winding down.

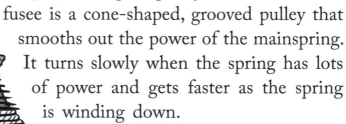

The design of the fusee evened out the mainspring's power, but spring-driven clocks and watches still weren't very accurate. The very best clocks were off by only one minute a day, but it was much more likely that a clock gained or lost as much as 15 minutes every day.

As the 1500s drew to a close, owning personal timepieces and having clocks in the home were considered status symbols. Members of the middle class, such as merchants, bankers, and lawyers, could afford to buy their own clocks or watches.

SWINGING FOR THE FENCES

In the 1630s, the Italian inventor and astronomer Galileo Galilei noticed that lamps hanging on chains from the ceiling of his church took the same amount of time to swing back and forth no matter how far the lamp moved. Puzzling, isn't it? Common sense would suggest that if one lamp swings 5 feet in an arc and another lamp swings 15 feet, the lamp that swings 15 feet should take three times as long because it covers three times as much distance.

Galileo tested his observation many times before concluding that swinging objects can cover different distances in the same amount of time.

Galileo Galilei

But why? The key discovery was that any weight on a rope or chain doesn't just swing on the rope. It actually falls first, and the rope catches it and pulls it along. As a lamp falls, it picks up speed. A lamp falling a larger distance swings faster than a lamp that doesn't fall as far. The faster speed of a longer fall makes up for the longer distance. So the travel time for both lamps is the same.

Is this an object that moves at a constant rate? Sounds like the start of a clock!

Did You Know?

Between 1300 and 1600, clockmakers used better and better materials and made smaller and smaller gears to fit into pocket watches and other devices. But the basic design didn't change all that much. An unwinding rope, which was repeatedly stopped and released by a verge escapement, turned a bunch of gears that turned an arm around a dial or rang bells.

pendulum: an object that swings freely in an arc by force of **gravity**.

gravity: a force that pulls objects to the earth.

Galileo then discovered that what matters most to the speed of a swinging object is the length of the cord holding it—the longer the cord, the longer it takes for the object to complete an entire arc. By adjusting the length of the cord, an object could be made to swing at exactly the rate needed to move the gears of a clock. Galileo sketched out a design for a **pendulum** clock in 1637, although he never had a chance to build it.

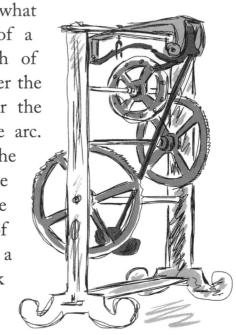

Galileo Galilei

Galileo Galilei (1564–1642) was born in Pisa, Italy. He was a mathematician and astronomer who researched the theory of motion—how objects fall and move through space. One of Galileo's most famous findings is that all objects fall at the same speed. There is a story that Galileo proved this by dropping two balls of different weights from the Leaning Tower of Pisa, but this story is most likely untrue.

In 1609, Galileo heard about a remarkable spyglass that let a person see distant objects as if they were close. He built his own telescope, and within a year he made many fantastic discoveries: he saw mountains on the moon, found out that the Milky Way was made up of stars, spotted four moons around Jupiter, and noted that Venus had phases like Earth's moon. These findings were evidence that the earth wasn't at the center of the universe, as many people believed. It helped to prove that the earth and all the other planets revolved around the sun, as astronomer Nicolas Copernicus had argued nearly a century earlier.

In 1656, unaware of Galileo's findings and design, the Dutch scientist Christian Huygens built a pendulum clock of his own. He used the pendulum to time the movement of the escapement. If left alone, the pendulum would eventually slow down and stop moving. But Huygens designed his clock so that the movement of the escapement gave the pendulum a little push with each swing.

Huygens' pendulum was a great idea, but it didn't work quite right with the verge escapement. The solution to the problem was the **anchor escapement**, which was invented by another scientist about 15 years later. Named after its shape, the anchor escapement swings back and forth in much less space than the verge escapement. The shorter distance makes the pendulum more accurate.

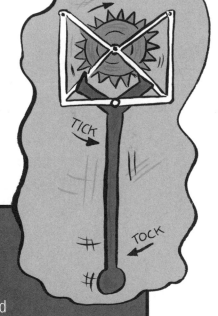

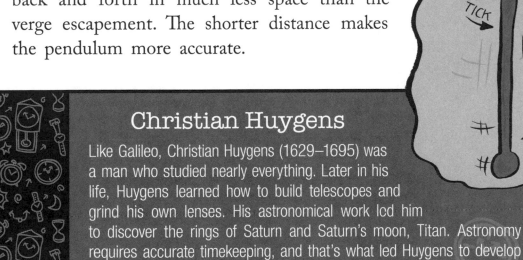

Christian Huygens

Like Galileo, Christian Huygens (1629–1695) was a man who studied nearly everything. Later in his life, Huygens learned how to build telescopes and grind his own lenses. His astronomical work led him to discover the rings of Saturn and Saturn's moon, Titan. Astronomy requires accurate timekeeping, and that's what led Huygens to develop the pendulum clock.

THE LONGITUDE PROBLEM

The pendulum clock worked well on land, but it was no better on ships than clocks made with verge escapements. Without accurate clocks, ship captains had trouble determining their **longitude** at sea.

While latitude measures how far a location is north or south of the equator, longitude measures how far a location is east or west of a fixed point. This fixed point is called the **prime meridian** and it marks 0 degrees longitude. Like latitude, longitude is measured in degrees, and 360 degrees of longitude make one complete trip around the earth.

Since the earth is about 24,900 miles around at the equator (38,620 kilometers), each degree of longitude is at most 70 miles wide (112 kilometers). This is figured by dividing the distance around the earth by the number of degrees in a circle (because the earth is round): 24,900 ÷ 360 = 69.16. Near the North or South Pole, however, a degree of longitude might be only 10 miles wide (16 kilometers)! Can you see why this is true? Look at a globe. The **circumference** of the earth is widest at the equator and narrowerst at the poles.

It was important for sailors to know that traveling 15 degrees of longitude to the east moves local time ahead one hour. This is because 360 degrees divided by 24 hours equals 15 degrees per hour. Traveling 15 degrees west moves local time back one hour.

WORDS TO KNOW

longitude: imaginary lines running from the North Pole to the South Pole around the globe.

prime meridian: the imaginary line running through Greenwich, England, that divides the world into the Eastern Hemisphere and Western Hemisphere.

circumference: the distance around the outside of a circle or globe.

X > Y

English sailors knew how to find their latitude, track their speed, and find the local time. But they needed to know the time in a fixed location, and this is where it all went wrong. They tried to keep a clock on board that was set to local time in Greenwich, England, but conditions at sea and changes in temperature made the clocks inaccurate. This put sailors in constant danger. If they didn't know their location, they couldn't navigate accurately. In 1707, for example, four ships were wrecked on England's Isles of Scilly, killing more than 2,000 sailors.

For an island nation like England, the ability to navigate was important.

Where Am I?

If you know the local times at two points and the location of one point, you can figure out the location of the other point. To understand how this works, imagine that you ride for an hour in a car without a mileage indicator, but you need to know how many miles you drove. How will you do it? Look at what you do know:

- Your starting point, because you left from there.

- The time you left the starting point, because you looked at the clock.

- The current time, because you looked at the clock.

- The speed that you drove, because you looked at the speedometer.

With all this information, you can figure out how many miles you are from the starting point because you know how long you drove and at what speed.

- Current time − Time you left = Drive time.

- Drive time × Speed = Distance from your starting point.

If you also looked at a compass while you rode, you'd even be able to figure out your exact current location!

Timekeeping

To encourage scientists to solve the longitude problem, in 1714 the British Parliament offered a 20,000-pound reward (equal to millions of dollars today). The reward was offered for a **chronometer** clock that kept time accurately enough that sailors could tell where they were on the ocean within a half-degree of longitude. The Board of Longitude was created to evaluate the inventions.

WORDS TO KNOW

chronometer: a very accurate timepiece, used in navigation to determine longitude.

grasshopper escapement: an escapement used in pendulum clocks that jumped between the teeth of a wheel.

It took decades to name a winner of the reward. John Harrison, who had taught himself science and clock making, designed his first clock in 1715 at the age of 23. He built many timekeeping devices, including a clock made entirely of wood that is still running to this day. He invented an entirely new escapement called the **grasshopper escapement**. Harrison's clocks were so accurate that the best of them were off by one second per month at most.

In 1730, after many years of work on different clock designs, Harrison met with Edmund Halley, the discoverer of Halley's Comet, and George Graham, the country's leading clockmaker. Graham was highly impressed by Harrison and lent him money so that Harrison could spend the next five

John Harrison

years working on what was known as Harrison-1, or H-1. The clock was tested when Harrison and H-1 sailed round-trip to Lisbon, Portugal. On the way home, Harrison's clock let the captain know that he was more than 60 miles west of where he thought he was (96 kilometers)!

Harrison went back to the Board of Longitude and asked for more money to make a clock as good as H-1 but smaller. Harrison-2 withstood extreme temperatures and violent shaking, but it was too heavy, so Harrison started work on H-3.

After 20 years, Harrison realized H-3 was never going to work, so he started on something new. Within two years he produced H-4, one of the smallest navigation clocks ever made, at only 5 inches in diameter (12½ centimeters).

When H-4 was tested on an 81-day trip to Jamaica in 1761, the clock lost a total of five seconds on the trip.

Harrison was clearly the most skilled clockmaker in England and possibly the world, yet he had to wait another 11 years before being paid by King George III. Why the long wait? British scientists who hoped to win the prize themselves argued that Harrison got lucky with H-4, because there was no way a clock that small could be accurate.

Did You Know?

To prove that H-4 worked, Harrison had to hand over details on the clock, create another from scratch, and let another clockmaker use his design to create yet another copy.

Harrison recommended Larcum Kendall to build a copy of H-4. Captain Cook used Kendall's K-1 during a three-year voyage to Antarctica and it was never off by more than eight seconds during the entire trip. King George himself tested the clock in 1772, and the following year, Harrison was finally awarded the prize money and recognized as the one who solved the longitude problem.

ACTIVITY

LOOKING FOR LONGITUDE

Supplies

- Internet access
- 2 clocks
- sundial
- sunny day
- paper and pencil

You've already learned how to use a quadrant to determine your latitude. Now it's time to find your longitude.

1 Find out what time it is in Greenwich, England. This is called **Greenwich Mean Time**. Visit Greenwichmeantime.com for the exact time in Greenwich, to the second. Set one clock to this time.

Greenwich Mean Time (GMT): the solar time at the Royal Observatory in Greenwich, England, located at 0 degrees longitude.

2 At midday wherever you are, set the other clock to noon when the sun is directly overhead. To find out when noon happens locally—and not just noon in your time zone—use a sundial. Wait until the shadow of the gnomon is directly in line with the gnomon itself.

3 Now compare the two clocks. By how much time do they differ? The earth rotates about 15 degrees per hour, so if the clocks differ by exactly 6 hours, then you are either 90 degrees west or 90 degrees east of Greenwich. (15 degrees × 6 hours = 90 degrees.) What if the clocks differ by, say, 6 hours and 20 minutes? You know that 20 minutes is one-third of an hour, which is the same as 0.33 of an hour. Then you multiply 15 degrees by 6.33 hours.

Here is the longitude for a few places you may know of:

- Reykjavík, Iceland: 22°W
- New York, New York: 73°W
- Chicago, Illinois: 88°W
- San Francisco, California: 122°W
- Honolulu, Hawaii: 157°W
- Paris, France: 2°E
- Cairo, Egypt: 31°E
- New Delhi, India: 77°E
- Beijing, China: 116°E
- Sydney, Australia: 151°E

Did You Know?

The International Date Line is an imaginary line where 180 degrees west meets 180 degrees east. If you look at a map you'll see why the line zigs and zags through the Pacific Ocean—to avoid going through any land. On the west side of the line it is one day later than on the east side of the line.

ACTIVITY

PUTTING PENDULUM POWER TO THE TEST

Much has changed since the time of Galileo, but the forces of physics remain the same. You can recreate Galileo's experiments with pendulums to see how they work.

Supplies

- 2 chairs, tables, or desks of the same height
- 4 rulers
- masking tape
- pieces of string, 15–20 inches long (37–50 centimeters)
- scissors
- timer
- 12 or more washers, at least as large as a nickel

1 Position the chairs or tables side by side, leaving a gap between them a little shorter than your shortest ruler.

2 To create supports for your pendulums, tape three of the rulers to the chairs or tables so that the rulers rest over the gap. Use the fourth ruler for measuring.

3 Tie one washer to one piece of string. Tape the loose end to one of the rulers so that the string is exactly 10 inches long (25 centimeters). Repeat this process with another string and ruler to create two identical pendulums.

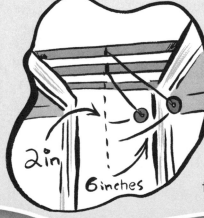

2 in
6 inches

4 Pull one washer back 2 inches (5 centimeters) and another washer back 6 inches (15 centimeters). Release them at the same time, and pay attention to when the strings are straight up and down. Are they vertical at the same time?

5 Play around with the length of string and the amount of weight on the string to see what causes a pendulum to swing faster or slower. How many washers do you need to add or how short must you make the string to make a pendulum swing twice as fast? Can you add weight and lengthen the string without changing the speed?

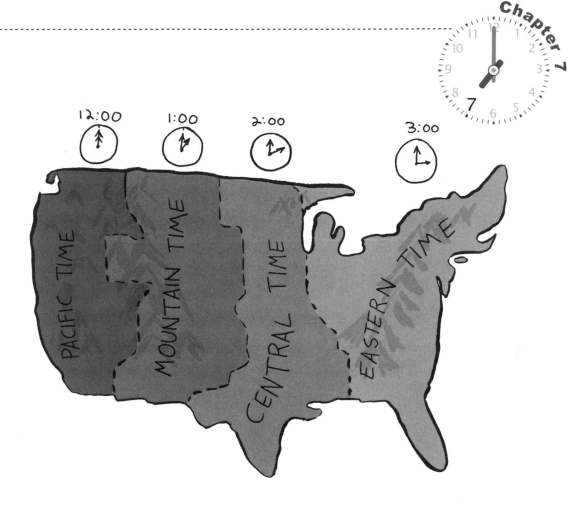

Chapter 7

SLICING THE WORLD INTO TIME ZONES

The effort to create accurate timekeeping devices ignores the fact that many units of time are completely random. Weeks, hours, seconds—we created them to help us organize our lives, but there's nothing physically real about them. We can't say, "Look, Ma! That's the third second we've spotted on this trip!"

Did you know that people have even argued about the definition of a day? This is because a day can be measured at least two different ways. One way is to measure the time that passes between noon and noon. This **solar day** is the one used most often. Another way is to measure how long it takes the earth to rotate once on its axis. This **sidereal day** gets its name from the Latin word *sidus* for star. A sidereal day passes when, from a location on Earth, a fixed star or constellation appears overhead twice in a row.

WORDS TO KNOW

solar day: the time it takes for the earth to make one complete rotation, measured against the sun.

sidereal day: the time it takes the earth to make one complete rotation, measured against a fixed star.

orbit: the path of an object circling another object in space.

Do you think a solar day sounds equal to a sidereal day?

These days might seem to be equal at first, but the solar day is longer than the sidereal day by almost four minutes. This is because the earth moves a little in its **orbit** around the sun during the time it takes to spin once on its axis. The curve of the orbit adds time so the earth needs to turn a little more than a full circle for one solar day. One rotation with respect to the stars takes 23 hours, 56 minutes, while one rotation with respect to the sun takes 24 hours.

Did You Know? Over a whole year the extra time in a solar day adds up to the stars making one more loop around the sky than the sun. So there is one extra sidereal day in a year.

AN HOUR BEGINS . . . WHEN?

Even though an hour is a made-up period of time, most people agree how long an hour lasts. The problem in the 1800s, though, was that not everyone agreed on when the hour started.

Pendulum clocks lost less than a minute per day, so the accuracy of the clocks wasn't the issue. But most people set their clocks at noon, and noon happened at a different time in almost every town. After all, the sun is directly overhead in Boston before it's overhead in New York.

The United States had about 300 different time zones.

Every large city set its own time based on when the sun was overhead. So when the clock read noon in Chicago, it was 12:24 p.m. in Cleveland; 12:13 p.m. in Cincinnati; 12:09 p.m. in Louisville, Kentucky; 11:50 a.m. in St. Louis; and 11:48 a.m. in Dubuque, Iowa.

In the early 1800s, when families traveled by stagecoach and wagon, having different times in different cities wasn't a big problem. Since traveling from New York to Boston took an entire day, it didn't matter if you lost 15 minutes on the way. When you arrived, you just looked for the nearest church tower and reset your watch.

Watching the Stars, Counting the Hours

Sailors started getting lost in large numbers in the late 1400s, when they sailed out of the Mediterranean Sea and began exploring the oceans. Christopher Columbus thought he had reached the Indian Ocean because he couldn't track longitude. He had no idea of the world's actual size.

Slowly sailors began to understand the true size of the world, but no one was able to figure out a practical solution to finding longitude. Around 1600, Spain and Holland offered huge rewards to anyone who could solve the longitude problem. Within a decade, Galileo offered a solution based on his recent discovery of Jupiter's four moons. The moons regularly crossed into Jupiter's shadow and disappeared from view, and Galileo tracked these movements so that anyone could determine the time in Europe by viewing these moons.

This solution would have worked if sailors could use telescopes on moving ships and keep watch of the moons until they saw exactly when a moon traveled into Jupiter's shadow. A similar solution proposed that a sailor could use the position of Earth's moon among the stars to determine time in England. King Charles II liked the idea, but was shocked to find that England's astronomers didn't know enough about the movement of these heavenly bodies.

LET'S SEE, I'd SAY... IT'S ABOUT MIDNIGHT.

King Charles II founded the Royal Observatory, Greenwich in London, England, in 1675. Its mission was to track the sun, moon, and planets, and create accurate star catalogs. The king hoped that this would help British ships to sail safely throughout the world.

Within a century England would have the accurate chronometer built by John Harrison. Over the decades the Royal Observatory came to symbolize time in England and, thanks to sea charts sold to sailors from other countries, throughout the world.

But hundreds of local times did cause trouble for long-distance train travel. If a train travels from Atlanta to Birmingham to New Orleans, for example, which times should be listed on the train schedule? The local time in each city? If so, then you need a separate clock on the train to track each of those times. But how long does the actual train ride take? That would require yet another clock.

Rather than track the time in each city, railroad companies decided to keep **railway time**. Having only one time across the entire country made it easier for the railroads. But anyone who traveled by train still had to figure out what railway time equaled in local time.

The invention of the *telegraph* helped railway companies *synchronize* their clocks from coast to coast.

In 1847, the British government passed a law that required all railroads to use Greenwich Mean Time (GMT), the time kept by the Royal Observatory. Within eight years, 98 percent of all public clocks in Great Britain were set to GMT.

WORDS TO KNOW

railway time: a standard time used by railroads that stayed the same, regardless of location.

telegraph: a communication system that transmits electric impulses through wires, usually in Morse code.

synchronize: to set watches to the same time.

T|mekeeping

In 1870, Professor Charles Dowd proposed a new system that would divide the United States into four vertical time zones, with each zone being 15 degrees in longitude wide. Remember, the earth rotates 360 degrees each day, and if you divide 360 by 24 hours, you get 15 degrees per hour.

Dowd's system was put into place on Sunday, November 18, 1883, a day that came to be known as "the day of the two noons." When the "new" noon arrived in each time zone, the U.S. Naval Observatory in Washington, DC. telegraphed the time across the country. Any town east of the middle of a time zone had already experienced noon once. With the adoption of the Eastern, Central, Mountain, and Pacific time zones, the clocks in these towns struck noon once again.

While most people accepted the new time zones, some felt that changing the time to accommodate the needs of businesses (specifically railroads) was an insult to their religious beliefs. They argued that it was unnatural to change the way time had always been recorded.

$15° = 1$ HOUR

Charles Dowd

Try, Try Again

Charles Dowd, a high school principal and professor of mathematics, is known as the father of time zones in the United States. But he wasn't the first American to suggest a longitudinal solution to the problem of hundreds of local time zones.

Back in 1809, amateur astronomer William Lambert recommended that Congress establish a prime meridian—that is, a longitude of degree 0—through Washington. He argued that our use of another country's prime meridian was "degrading" and "an encumbrance unworthy of the freedom and sovereignty of the American people and their government."

Along with this new prime meridian would come time zones 15 degrees wide. Congress rejected this proposal. One critic called Lambert's idea "useless" because creating a new prime meridian would force thousands of sailors to buy new maps!

Dowd had a much more practical goal than Lambert. He just wanted to make travel easy for everyone. With his time zone proposal in hand, he visited railway managers across the country in 1870 to see what they thought about the idea.

In 1872, Dowd issued a new plan to take account of everyone's suggestions. With the railroads supporting Dowd, it was only a matter of time before the country made his time zones a reality.

MY PROPOSAL WOULD...

Nope!

TIME ZONES

William Lambert

ZONING OUT

In 1884, one year after the United States split into time zones, representatives from 25 countries met in Washington, DC, to decide how to track time around the world. After much debate, they decided to expand Charles Dowd's system to the entire globe, slicing the earth into vertical, one-hour-wide time zones, each 15 degrees in longitude.

T|mekeeping

Everyone at the conference knew that global time zones were a good idea, but they were divided on where the prime meridian, the line of 0 degrees longitude, should be located. Historically, the French had placed 0 degrees longitude at the Paris Observatory, while the British had placed it at the Royal Observatory, and so forth.

In the end, much to the disappointment of the French, the conference placed the prime meridian through the Royal Observatory Greenwich.

Did You Know?

The equator, where the earth is the widest, is an obvious place to set at o degrees latitude. No one questions that the North Pole is 90 degrees north, and the South Pole is 90 degrees south. But you can place o degrees longitude on any vertical line on the globe and have the system work.

Greenwich had been issuing annual charts of the stars' movement for more than 100 years, which made Greenwich well-known by world travelers.

When it's noon in Greenwich, it's noon almost everywhere 7.5 degrees east or west of Greenwich as well. Exceptions are France and Spain, which are at the same longitude as Greenwich but match their clocks to those of Germany, Italy, and most of Europe. If you move west from Greenwich, the time will be one hour earlier for each 15 degrees you travel. If you move east, the time is one hour later. When it's 1 p.m. in Greenwich, the time is 5 a.m. in Los Angeles and 2 p.m. in Munich, Germany.

WORDS TO KNOW

daylight saving time (DST): shifting the clock in the spring to gain an extra hour of daylight in the evening.

Of course, *daylight saving time* throws a wrench into this well-timed machine.

Keep in mind that not all time zones are created equal. In the barren western areas of Russia, for example, many of the time zones are 30 degrees wide. This means that you skip two hours when going from one to another.

The International Date Line

There was one small problem with the original system of time zones. If the time in Greenwich is 1 p.m. on Tuesday and you travel 12 time zones west, losing an hour for each zone, the local time is 1 a.m. Tuesday. If, however, you travel 12 time zones east, gaining an hour for each zone, the local time is 1 a.m. Wednesday.

Clearly something is wrong here. If you travel 12 time zones west from Greenwich on a jet and your friend travels east on a similar jet, your friend will not show up one day ahead of you. The two of you will arrive at the same time on the same day!

As with the switch to the Gregorian calendar, the confusion results from our attempt to label time, not from the passing of time itself. To solve this dilemma, the 180-degree line of longitude was named the International Date Line. If you cross this line headed west, you jump ahead one day while keeping the hours and minutes the same. If you cross the line going east, you lose one day.

T|mekeeping

Iran, India, Afghanistan, and parts of Australia all have half time zones, so that when it's 1 p.m. in Greenwich, the time is 4:30 p.m. in Tehran and 6:30 p.m. in Bombay. Nepal is even trickier—it has its own time zone that's 5 hours and 45 minutes ahead of Greenwich.

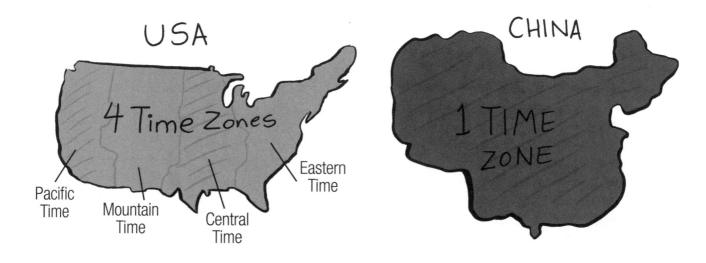

USA

4 Time Zones

Pacific Time
Mountain Time
Central Time
Eastern Time

CHINA

1 TIME ZONE

China spreads across 60 degrees of longitude and could have five time zones, but the Chinese government chooses to use only one time zone for the entire country.

This means the sun reaches its peak over the eastern part of the country at 11 a.m., while those in the west don't see "noon" until 3 p.m. This is exactly the situation that the United States chose to avoid. The working day for people living in western China starts long before sunrise, but some people choose to work untraditional hours so they don't have to get up in the middle of the night.

In reality, the lines marking the time zones zigzag back and forth along the borders of countries, states, and cities as they go from the North Pole to the South Pole. They can do this because people created them.

Countries can decide what's best for them in a time zone and change it if it doesn't work.

Although the first daylight saving time was in 1916, the idea dates back to 1784, when Benjamin Franklin wrote about moving hours around in an essay called "An Economical Project." It was before our lights were powered by electricity, when lamps burned oil.

Did You Know? Before 1995, the International Date Line ran down the middle of the country of Kiribati. The eastern part of the country was one day and two hours behind the western part, which included the capital. In 1995, Kiribati shifted the International Date Line east so that the entire country would finally be on the same day.

Discussion about the cost of oil led Franklin to write about how money could be saved if everyone went to bed earlier and woke up earlier. This would allow them to take advantage of the long daylight hours in spring and summer. With daylight saving we just move the hands of the clock ahead in the spring. And people do go to bed earlier! Perhaps Ben Franklin had the right idea.

Benjamin Franklin

Time Saved Is a Penny Earned

Benjamin Franklin (1706–1790) might be best known for the sayings that he created for *Poor Richard's Almanack*. Have you ever heard the saying, "A penny saved is a penny earned?" This is one of Benjamin Franklin's sayings. But you might not know about some of Franklin's other contributions to the American colonies and the new country.

Franklin was a publisher, scientist, diplomat, and inventor. Throughout the 1730s and 1740s, Franklin organized campaigns to light, clean, and pave the streets of Philadelphia. He organized the city's first library and first volunteer firefighting company. He invented bifocals, swim fins, and a heat-efficient stove, now called the Franklin stove. In the 1750s, he experimented with electricity and discovered the true nature of lightning.

Franklin helped write the Declaration of Independence and the U.S. Constitution. Today, the memory of Benjamin Franklin is still honored through his presence on the $100 bill and the number of U.S. towns named "Franklin."

IF I COULD SAVE TIME IN A BOTTLE . . .

Once everyone saw that the world didn't end when clocks changed to match the new time zones, they became a little more comfortable with the idea of moving time around. The next big change came when Germany and Austria set their clocks ahead by one hour during the summer of 1916. The countries wanted to preserve fuel during World War I, and shifting the clocks moved an hour of sunlight from the morning to the evening.

This meant that people used less electricity to light their homes.

Over the next year, most of the other European nations, as well as Australia and parts of Canada, also moved their clocks forward. The United States enacted a daylight saving law in 1918, but the government repealed the law after the end of World War I because most people didn't like it. Massachusetts, Rhode Island, and a few cities including New York, Chicago, and Philadelphia continued daylight saving time (DST) anyway during the summer months.

Did You Know?

Daylight saving time used to be known as "war time." This is because it was originally created to save fuel and energy during times of war.

Daylight saving time returned to the United States from 1942 to 1945 to help save fuel and energy in World War II.

Once the war ended, the government got rid of the law once again, and states were free to either adopt daylight saving time or leave the clocks alone.

Unfortunately, some states adopted DST and others left their clocks alone. This plunged the nation once again into a hodgepodge of local times, something time zones were designed to end. Businesses begged for a solution to the confusion, but they didn't always want the same solution.

DON'T FORGET DST TIME!

YOU MEAN "WAR TIME"?

Indoor theater owners, for example, argued for DST, while owners of drive-in theaters naturally wanted no DST so the sky would be darker earlier.

The solution finally came in 1966 when Congress passed the Uniform Time Act, which started DST nationwide at 2 a.m. on the final Sunday in April and ended it at 2 a.m. on the final Sunday in October.

In 2007, as a way to save energy across the country, the United States government changed the start date for DST to the second Sunday in March. It moved the end date for DST to the first Sunday in November.

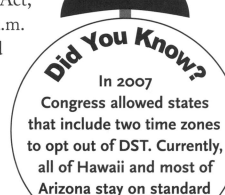

Did You Know?

In 2007 Congress allowed states that include two time zones to opt out of DST. Currently, all of Hawaii and most of Arizona stay on standard time all year.

To Switch or Not to Switch

In 2005, the state of Maine considered switching from the Eastern Standard Time Zone to the Atlantic Standard Time Zone. This would make Maine one hour earlier all the time, like staying on daylight saving time year-round. Since Maine is the easternmost state on Eastern Time, it gets less evening daylight than any other state. The feeling was that by shifting more daylight from the morning to the evening, people in Maine would save money on energy and be able to pursue outdoor activities later in the day. But it would mean that Maine would be an hour ahead of everyone else in the country for half the year. In the end, the state decided not to change time zones.

ACTIVITY

WHAT A DIFFERENCE A DAY MAKES

You can use coins to see how solar and sidereal days differ.

Supplies
- 1 quarter
- 1 penny

1 Place the coins face up on a table. The picture of George on the quarter (the sun) and the picture of Abe on the penny (the earth) should stare at one another, eye to eye.

2 Turn Abe counterclockwise one complete turn until he faces the same direction. This equals one rotation of the earth on its axis. To include the earth's movement around the sun, move Abe a bit counterclockwise around George without rotating Abe any further.

3 Since Abe faces the same direction, he sees the same background of stars behind the sun that he did to begin with. This counts as a sidereal day—one complete rotation of the earth, bringing the same stars directly overhead. But Abe no longer looks directly at George. To stare at the Founding Father, Abe must rotate just a tiny bit more counterclockwise. This extra bit of rotation, nearly 4 minutes worth in the case of Earth, completes one solar day.

87

Chapter 8

CRYSTAL CLEAR TIMEKEEPING

Clocks and watches at the beginning of the twentieth century were incredibly accurate compared to the shadow clocks and clepsydras of ancient times. But horologists thought they could still make improvements.

After all, anything with moving parts eventually breaks down. Ride a bicycle every day for 50 miles and at some point the chain will come off. The more you drive a car, the greater the chance of getting a flat tire. Clocks have to do their thing night and day without a rest, so it's no surprise that springs come unsprung.

frequency: the number of times an event occurs in a specific amount of time.

To make clocks work even better, horologists turned away from gears and pendulums. They found inspiration from an entirely new source: electricity. Of course, electricity itself wasn't new—lightning bolts had been striking the earth's surface for millions of years. But scientists kept discovering new facts about how it interacted with the rest of the world.

Around 1880, French scientists Pierre and Jacques Curie found that if you run an electric current through certain types of crystal, the crystal rapidly vibrates at a steady pace. By cutting the crystal in a particular shape, the brothers made it vibrate at a particular *frequency*.

Quartz crystals could be especially good for timekeeping since they vibrated at almost exactly the same rate— roughly 100,000 times per second—no matter what the temperature or air pressure.

Did You Know? The quartz design proved to be incredibly accurate. The quartz clock installed in the Royal Observatory in 1939 kept time accurately to within two-one-thousandths of a second per day. This is less than one second of error over an entire year.

Pierre and Marie Curie

Pierre Curie was devoted to figuring out how the world worked. After discovering **piezoelectricity** with his brother Jacques, Pierre Curie went on to study magnetism. He found that at a certain temperature, a substance loses its magnetic properties. This is called the **Curie point** or Curie temperature of a substance.

In 1895, Curie married Marie Sklodowska, and they spent much of the next decade studying **radioactivity**. In addition to creating the word "radioactive" to label substances like uranium, the Curies discovered two new radioactive substances: radium and polonium.

Today, we know that handling radium can make you very sick and cause cancer, but the Curies didn't know that. Pierre carried radium around in his coat pocket so that he could show friends what he was working on. Marie even kept a small pile of radium salt by her bed because she liked the way it glowed at night.

Marie and Pierre Curie

WORDS TO KNOW

piezoelectricity: the electric current carried by quartz crystals.

Curie point: the temperature at which a substance loses its magnetism.

radioactivity: the emission of a stream of particles or electromagnetic rays.

Joseph W. Horton and Warren A. Marrison first came up with the idea of using quartz crystals to make a clock in 1928, but quartz clocks didn't actually appear until the late 1930s. To turn the vibrations of quartz into a timekeeping device, the electronic components of the clock or watch make the vibrations larger, without changing the frequency. The electronics send a signal to the display each time the count passes 100,000 or so. In a quartz watch with hands, the electronics make a pulse each second, which drives a tiny motor, and this motor turns gears that drive the hands.

Like the first mechanical clocks that used escapements, early quartz clocks were huge and expensive. So while the timekeeping was very accurate, few people could afford these clocks.

Finally, in the 1970s manufacturers figured out how to make a quartz design run on less power. Once they did this, they could fit the battery and quartz crystals into a small wristwatch.

In later years, manufacturers learned to fit more power into even less space. Quartz watches started featuring calculators, alarms, stopwatches, and other features.

Analog quartz watches still have gears that use the quartz vibrations to move the hour, minute, and second hands. But they have fewer moving parts than older analog watches that used a balance spring and winding stem. Fewer moving parts means less friction and fewer opportunities to break—an important advance from past designs.

Digital quartz watches, which became available in the 1970s, use *circuits* to translate the quartz vibrations into an electronic display of the time. With no moving parts other than the vibrating quartz, they are extremely reliable. You can only see the vibrations of a quartz crystal with a high-powered microscope.

WORDS TO KNOW

analog: presenting data as a measurable physical quality.

circuit: a path for electric current to flow, beginning and ending at the same point.

T|mekeeping

Digital or Analog?

An example of a digital clock is the standard bedside alarm clock with glowing red numbers. They flash 12:00 when the power comes back on after it has gone off. An analog clock might have a face with moving arms that point to the current hour, minute, and second. These clocks clearly differ from one another, but it's not that all digital clocks are electric while all analog clocks are not. Many clocks with faces are plugged into an electric outlet, yet they're still analog.

The real difference comes in how a clock displays the time to a viewer. With a digital clock, time is displayed discontinuously. This means that it appears in separate pieces, with breaks. The bedside clock reads 9:13 for a while, then suddenly changes to 9:14. You can't see how many seconds have passed while you wait for the minute to change. Digital clocks can be more detailed, showing seconds, tenths of seconds, and so on. But no matter how detailed you get, the clock still jumps from one reading of time to another.

Analog is the opposite of digital, which means that an analog clock displays time in a continuous manner. As you watch the hands on an analog clock, you can see time pass before your eyes. If you watch for a while, you will see the hour hand move slowly from one number to another. The minute and second hands move more quickly, but by looking closely, you can see when it's 15 minutes and three seconds past 4 o'clock and when it's 15 minutes and three-and-one-half seconds past 4 o'clock.

If you think about the timekeeping devices discussed in this book, you'll realize that most of them are analog. Shadow clocks, sundials, nocturnals, clepsydras, candle clocks, incense, and pendulum clocks all display time continuously as the sun moves, water flows, and wax melts.

Interestingly, while the sandglass is analog, it could be turned into a digital clock. How? Take the sandglass apart and count the number of grains of sand. Then put it back together with a device that counts the grains as they fall. If the device displays the number of grains that have fallen, you now have a digital clock!

WHEN EVERY SECOND
(AND TENTH OF A SECOND) COUNTS

Athletic competition pits human against human in contests to see who can lift the most weight, who can throw an object the farthest, or who is fastest. Competition in sports like skiing, swimming, speed skating, running, and cycling are races to see who can reach the finish line in the shortest amount of time.

Some events might seem easy to compare. In the 100-meter dash, for instance, one person can fire a pistol to tell runners when to start running, while another person at the finish line can see who crosses it first. But what if two or more runners are very close? You might have a hard time seeing which one finished first.

In addition, we want to know more than which athlete is the fastest today. We want to know whether an athlete today is faster than the one who won the race last time, or last year, or 40 years ago. We like to compare the performances of athletes over time, and we can only do that by timing races and keeping records.

At the 2012 London Olympics, 450 professional timekeepers used the latest technology to measure running, swimming, and bicycling events. With 800 volunteers, 390 scoreboards, and over 110 miles of cables, timing at these Olympic Games was accurate to the nearest one-thousandth of a second—40 times quicker than the blink of an eye.

What happens if all the athletes in a race can't compete at the same time? In the first American downhill ski races, all the skiers started at the same time and the first one to reach the finish line won. Skiers could take any trail they wanted to get to the bottom. Eventually the racers decided this was unfair and a fixed course was developed. To make sure skiers didn't hurt one another, skiers started one after another. Race times were compared after everyone was finished.

For decades, starting with the 1912 Olympic Games in Stockholm, Sweden, the only timing device available to athletes was the stopwatch. An official would press one button to start the stopwatch and press another button to stop it when someone crossed the finish line. Unfortunately, this way of tracking time has two main problems.

First, to use a stopwatch, you have to be alert. If you sneeze at the start of the race, you might start the stopwatch late and make athletes seem a second or two faster than they really are. Secondly, human reaction time has definite limits. When you see someone cross the finish line, it takes a bit of time for your finger to press the button on the stopwatch. Another race official might be faster or slower than you, so you can't compare times accurately.

In the 1960s, American Jim Hines held the world record for the 100-meter dash at 9.9 seconds. At that time, stopwatches only measured tenths of a second, so Hines actually ran anywhere from 9.85 to 9.94 seconds. One-tenth of a second might not seem like much, but it's a big difference in a race that takes less than 10 seconds.

To solve these problems, race officials switched to computerized timing. The 1964 Olympics in Tokyo, Japan, marked the first use of an electronic touchpad in swimming competitions. To the naked eye, the German Hans-Joachim Klein and the American Gary Ilman appeared to tie for third place in the 100-meter freestyle event. The timing devices showed that Klein had touched the pad a thousandth of a second before Ilman, so Germany was awarded the bronze medal.

Did You Know? Until 2003, runners were allowed two false starts in a race. In 2003, this changed to one false start, and in 2010, no false starts. Usain Bolt, the men's world record holder in the 100-meter dash, was disqualified in the 2011 world championships because of a false start.

Timing devices are also used at the start of some events. In sprints like the 100-meter dash, runners start in a crouched position with their feet pressed against aluminum blocks. The blocks electronically record when the athletes' feet leave the blocks.

If anyone's feet leave within one-tenth of a second after the starting gun, the runner is immediately disqualified.

Our nerves and muscles aren't fast enough to respond within one-tenth of a second, so anyone who started running before then must have started before the gun actually fired.

TEST YOUR TIMING REFLEX

Supplies

- 2 digital stopwatches
- you and 2 friends

Here's how to test your reflexes—and see how difficult it is to time a race or other athletic event accurately using a hand-held stopwatch.

1 You and a friend each take a stopwatch. The other friend will be the starter.

2 When the starter says "Go!" start your stopwatch. When he or she says "Stop!" hit the stop button.

3 Now compare times with your friend. Are they the same? Are they exactly the same? Take turns being the starter and timers. Imagine what it would be like if you were an Olympic athlete and you just happened to be timed by someone with slower reflexes than anyone else—good-bye, gold medal.

4 Try this with races that rely on the timers watching for a beginning and an end point and see what happens. Are your times closer together or farther apart than when you listened for the start and stop commands?

GO!

STOP

Wow! OFF BY 0.5 SECONDS.

Chapter 9

Atomic Clock

MEASURING TIME WITHOUT MOVING

In the 1940s, quartz clocks were more accurate than any previous clock in human history. Within a decade, however, quartz was old news, thanks to the arrival of *atomic clocks*. These are extremely accurate timekeeping devices that are controlled by the vibrations of *atoms* or *molecules*.

Cesium-133

WORDS TO KNOW

atomic clock: an extremely accurate timekeeping device that is controlled by the vibrations of atoms or molecules.

atom: a small particle of matter.

molecule: a very small particle made of combinations of atoms.

cesium-133: a form of the element cesium whose vibrations are measured as a time standard.

hertz (Hz): cycles per second.

The first atomic clock was built in the United States in 1949. It relied on the vibrations of ammonia molecules to control an electronic signal that displayed the time. This clock was 10 times more accurate than a quartz clock. But in 1955, Britain's National Physical Laboratory built an atomic clock powered by **cesium-133** atoms. A cesium-133 atom vibrated more regularly and more frequently than an ammonia molecule.

In 1967, the World's Conference on Weights and Measures declared the vibrations of the cesium atom to be the world standard for measuring the second.

The cesium-133 atom vibrates at a frequency of 9,192,631,770 **hertz (Hz)**. When microwave energy has a frequency of exactly 9,192,631,770 Hz, any cesium atoms hit by the microwaves change to a different energy state. The changed cesium atoms reinforce the microwaves so that their frequency always remains at 9,192,631,770 Hz. Once this happens, another device within the clock translates this frequency into the familiar one beat per second.

Did You Know?

What's most amazing about this atomic clock is that it has an error rate of only one second every 300 years—which is actually more precise than the solar system itself!

How can a clock be more precise than the solar system?

Because the earth does not always move at the same rate as it orbits the sun. In fact, because the earth's orbit is an **ellipse** and not a circle, the earth moves faster when it's close to the sun and slower when it's far away.

The earth doesn't always spin on its axis at the same rate, either. Strong winds and the pressure of the **atmosphere** cause the earth to slow down. This is increasing the length of a day by a fraction of a **millisecond**. The daily movement of the tides is also slowing the earth by about 1.4 milliseconds per day over a 100-year period.

Those milliseconds actually add up over time. As scientists found out more about the movement of the earth and how it changes over time, they decided that they could no longer define a second as 1/86,400 of a solar day. A solar day is the period from noon to noon, and 86,400 seconds equals 1,440 minutes, which equals 24 hours. This just wasn't accurate enough.

ellipse: an oval shape.

atmosphere: the blanket of air surrounding the earth.

millisecond: one-thousandth of a second.

ALL ABOUT ATOMS

In other words, you can measure atoms more precisely than planets. This makes sense, if you think about it. After all, which can you measure more accurately: the length of your finger or a car, the height of a chair or the flagpole at your school? The longer, higher, or bigger something is, the more likely you are to make an error while measuring it—and it might not even be your fault. The wind might sway the flagpole, for instance, and that will throw off your accuracy.

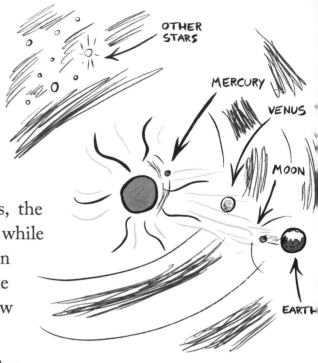

KEEP ON TICKING

A clock that loses or gains only one second over 300 years sounds pretty good, but for scientists it was only the beginning of 50 years of improvement. In 1975, NBS-6, an atomic clock run by the U.S. National Bureau of Standards (NBS), improved the error rate to one second every 300,000 years. By 1993, the National Institute of Standards and Technology (NIST—the new name for NBS) had created a clock 20 times better than NBS-6.

millennium bug: the inability of computer software and hardware to recognize the date when it changes centuries.

In 1999, while most of the world worried about their computers losing track of 100 years due to the **millennium bug**, NIST introduced NIST-F1, an atomic clock that measures the atoms so precisely, it would not gain or lose a second in more than 20 million years.

By 2010, the clock's accuracy had improved so that it would not be off by a second in more than 100 million years! Official United States government time is set by this clock.

Why do we need clocks this precise? Scientists often research subjects just because it is interesting and fun. They do the research first, then let other people worry about whether it's useful or not.

As it turns out, making very accurate clocks has allowed scientists and manufacturers to do all sorts of things that weren't possible before. Today's computer networks can "read" official atomic time over the Internet so they all have the correct time, which is important for proper communication between computers.

WORDS TO KNOW

galaxy: a collection of star systems held together by gravity.

quasar: an object in space that emits huge amounts of energy.

Global Positioning System (GPS): a system of satellites, computers, and receivers that determine the latitude and longitude of a receiver on earth by calculating the time difference for signals from different satellites to reach the receiver.

Astronomers use radio telescopes orbiting the earth to "see" far into the universe. Using atomic time, they link telescopes together for more accurate picture of **galaxies** and **quasars** billions of light years away.

GPS

An important use of atomic clocks is the **Global Positioning System (GPS)**, first launched in 1978. GPS was originally a set of 24 satellites that orbit the earth. Each satellite takes 12 hours to make a complete orbit, and they're arranged in space so that every point on the planet is always in radio contact with at least four satellites. In 2011, three more satellites were added to improve coverage.

As the signals travel toward Earth, they change frequency depending on where someone is in relation to the satellite. If the satellite is moving toward you, the radio signal will increase in frequency because it's covering slightly less ground to reach you and the waves are bunching together as they get close. Once the satellite passes overhead, its frequency will slightly decrease because as it moves away from you, the waves have room to stretch out.

This effect is called the Doppler shift. Maybe you have already experienced this change in frequency from listening to a fire engine or ambulance as it passed you on the street. As the vehicle approaches you, its siren or bell sounds like it's getting higher and higher. The moment it passes you, the sound drops lower and keeps falling.

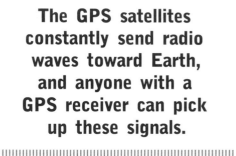

Did You Know?
In 1957, the Soviet Union launched *Sputnik*, the world's first satellite. Researchers at the Massachussetts Institute of Technology were able to calculate the satellite's orbit by tracking its Doppler shift.

Using Clocks to Improve Your Vision

To understand how clocks help scientists see better, hold your hand over one eye and look around the room. Everything will look flatter than normal because you're seeing it from only one angle. Uncover your eye and look again—the room should return to normal. What's happening is that your brain takes the images from the two eyes and blends them into one, letting you more accurately judge how far away different objects are.

Now imagine that your internal clock isn't working right, and your right eye processes information one second slower than the left. If you try to play baseball, you'll see two images of the ball because you're seeing them at different times.

While you're limited to using information from two eyes, astronomers can use any number of radio telescopes as long as the information they see comes at the exact same point in time. Atomic clocks allow this level of precision. Astronomers have been able to link 10 telescopes between Hawaii and the Virgin Islands to create, in effect, a 5,000-mile-wide telescope (8,000 kilometers). This allows astronomers to learn more about the parts of the universe farthest away from us.

The U.S. Navy used the idea of tracking Doppler shift when it launched a satellite navigation system in 1965. The six satellites in the Transit System sent radio signals to American submarines carrying nuclear missiles. The system provided the submarines with such accurate signals that the subs were able to stay submerged in the ocean for months at a time—something they couldn't previously do without getting far off course.

The U.S. Department of Defense then wanted to try something bigger, something that would cover the entire world.

Timekeeping

The first 24 GPS satellites were launched between 1978 and 1993. Each weighs about 1,900 pounds and carries four atomic clocks on board. GPS first gained wide public attention in the 1991 Gulf War, when U.S. troops used GPS to find their way through the deserts of the Middle East and target bombs accurately.

Like many technological innovations that were first developed for the military, GPS is now used in other ways:

• **Drivers** use GPS to find their location and destination. GPS systems even speak directions and provide drivers with live traffic updates. Boat owners use GPS to help them navigate.

• **Police** find stolen cars using their GPS systems.

• **Airlines** use GPS to make flight paths more direct, and pilots can make safer landings because they know their exact position in the air.

• **Pet owners** can use a tiny GPS tag placed under the skin of their pet to locate a lost animal.

• **Scientists** can track animal migration to study animal behavior.

The Next Clock

In 2012 the most accurate clock is an NIST optical clock in Boulder, Colorado. It keeps time to within 1 second in 3.7 billion years. Optical clocks use light rather than the microwaves used by atomic clocks. But the use of this incredibly precise clock is limited by the system used to communicate time around the globe. Scientists in Germany have been able to send an optical clock signal over hundreds of kilometers, but until it can be communicated around the world, the optical clock cannot be used as an international time standard. For now, we are stuck with our atomic clock that keeps time to within 1 second in 100 million years for our official time.

ACTIVITY

- -

FINDING A QUARTER
IN A HAYSTACK

You can see for yourself how GPS works by getting together with three friends and performing a few experiments. If you need to entice them, tell them the experiment is all about finding money in a field.

1 Your friends get to play the role of the GPS satellites. Position them at the edges of a large grassy field. It should be about the size of a football field with long grass that hides the ground. Everyone should be roughly at equal distances from one another.

2 Have each person slowly walk around the field, looking toward the center of the field the entire time. At some point, throw a quarter so it lands in the middle of the field.

3 If the "satellites" have been doing their job, they'll be able to pool their information. Each person should offer some information about where the quarter landed, such as, "It landed to my left" or "It landed at least 15 feet in front of me." Using information from three different sources, you should be able to find the quarter together.

Not convinced? Have one person walk around the edge of the field and repeat the experiment. The "satellite" will have a general indication of where the coin landed, but will likely have to spend much more time searching for the coin. Try the experiment with two people, and with four people. If you time how long it takes each group to find the quarter, what can you conclude?

105

Chapter 10

TIME ON YOUR HANDS

By looking at the history and science of timekeeping, we have also learned about the history of time itself—what it is and isn't, and how time has become an essential part of our modern world. More importantly, we've gained an idea of how timekeeping and our ideas of time affect one another. If we divide a length of time a particular way—24 hours in a day, for example, or 60 seconds in a minute—we will design timekeeping devices to track those pieces.

If we create a timekeeping device that's more accurate than our current divisions—such as an atomic clock that counts cesium's 9,192,631,770 pulses—we will divide time into smaller pieces to match what we are capable of tracking.

Time is as much a tool in our lives as a hammer or a stapler, and we use time zones and daylight saving time to make time a more useful tool. We add days to calendars and leap seconds to the year. We manipulate time by setting our watch five minutes ahead so that we arrive at appointments early.

One time trick we haven't tried is a reorganization of our whole system—days, months, minutes, years, everything.

Why would we want to do that? Well, we divide a year into 365 pieces (and sometimes 366), months into 28–31 pieces, a day into 24 pieces, an hour into 60 pieces, and a second into hundreds or millions of pieces. No unit of time relates easily to another, so the system is hard to learn and even harder to calculate using our base 10 counting system. How many days is 1,000,000 minutes? How many years is 10,000 days? Better get out the calculator!

TWENTY-FIVE O'CLOCK

Measuring time doesn't have to be so complicated. For example, J. William Cupp, an associate professor of computer and information sciences at Indiana Wesleyan University, has proposed a system for metric time that makes counting much easier. He keeps the solar day and solar year but changes everything else. Under his system, the day is broken up into 25 hours with each hour having 100 minutes and each minute 100 seconds.

Timekeeping

If you do the math, our current system has 86,400 seconds in a day. Under Cupp's system, a day lasts 250,000 metric seconds, so each metric second is about one-third of a regular second. Similarly, each metric minute is about half of a regular minute.

Cupp did this so that adopting a metric time system would be fairly easy. If you microwave a bag of popcorn, set the timer for 8 minutes instead of 4. A 3-minute egg becomes a 6-minute egg without spending a moment longer in the water.

Like Marco Mastrofini (who we talked about in chapter one), Cupp also proposes a calendar in which every month starts on a Sunday so that people can use the same calendar every year instead of having to buy a new one. Each month would have 28 days, and a year would have 13 months, with one special New Year's Day that falls between December 28 and January 1.

Every Year Tells a Story

Chris Hardman, the artistic director of a theater company in Sausalito, California, created the "ECOlogical Calendar" to return to a better awareness of nature and the larger world. His calendar unfolds as one long sheet, beginning with the winter solstice, December 21, instead of January 1. In addition to using the standard names of the days, Hardman gives each day an individual name relating to the weather: February 17 is "FreezeSleep," while the next two days in February are named "ArcticAir" and "QuickCold."

The illustrations on the calendar show the seasons flowing into one another, and Hardman uses the names of the days to tell a story that emphasizes how the days and months flow together over time. For example, the sentence covering February 17–19 reads: "FreezeSleep comes to woolly bear caterpillars as ArcticAir blows toward the equator making QuickCold all things outside."

While it makes sense to have timekeeping be as easy as possible, changing over to Cupp's system would take a lot of work. Every watch and clock, every cell phone, and every calendar in the world would have to be changed.

A lot of work, yes, but we've taken on such projects before. In 1999, the world overhauled its computers to avoid the millennium bug that would crash every computer on January 1, 2000. And in 2002, 12 European countries—roughly 300 million people—adopted the Euro, an entirely new system of money.

In fact, in 1793, the French government used a metric time system for 13 years. The revised calendar had 12, three-week-long months, with each week having 10 days. Each solar day was broken into 10 metric hours, each hour into 100 metric minutes, and each minute into 100 metric seconds. Most of the metric system created during this time in France—meters, liters, and grams—has spread throughout the world, but metric time didn't make it.

What do you think? Should we keep the clunky, 24-hour clock that we all know and understand? Or switch to a funky new 25-hour system that would be easy to learn and make adding minutes and hours easier?

TIME FLIES

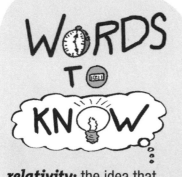

relativity: the idea that an object's movement and speed make sense only when compared with other objects.

As we go about our daily lives, physical objects, or things, don't normally affect how quickly or slowly time passes. If your living room clock stops working, time keeps on going. The clock doesn't create time but only measures it. Once you get the clock repaired, you can ask a neighbor for the time and reset your clock because time passes the same for your neighbor as it does for you.

Or does it? As Albert Einstein explained in his 1905 essay on **relativity**, the answer is sometimes no. Einstein's essay turned the world of science upside-down because it destroyed the idea of an "absolute time" that exists outside the physical happenings of the universe.

Einstein argued that everyone has his or her own personal time, and it's a time related to movement.

Einstein showed that time passes at the same rate for two people only if they are moving in the same direction and at the same speed. If the two people move at different speeds or in different directions or both, then their "personal clocks"—the rate at which time passes for each of them—will not necessarily match. Their clocks might differ by only the tiniest amount, but they will differ.

Seeker of Solar Secrets

Albert Einstein is the world's most famous scientist—despite the fact that most people can't understand what he discovered! Born in 1879 in Germany, Einstein lived in Italy and Switzerland when he was young. After finishing college, he published physics papers that threw the world of science into a tizzy. His theory of special relativity, which described how particles move when traveling near the speed of light, included the formula $E=mc^2$, which shows that energy is equal to mass multiplied by the speed of light (186,000 miles per second squared).

His second most famous paper introduced the theory of general relativity, which explained that acceleration (an increase in motion, such as when you push on the gas pedal) is equal to the force of gravity (the "pull" that large objects generate, such as the earth's pull on objects on its surface). If, for example, you rode on an extremely fast rocket ship, the speed of the ship would push you toward the back wall, just like the gravity of earth pushes you into the ground.

Albert Einstein

Believe it or not, this wacky-sounding idea has been proven in numerous experiments. In October 1971, for instance, cesium-based atomic clocks were flown around the world both from east to west and from west to east. Atomic clocks set to the same time were left in place at the U.S. Naval Observatory. After making the trips, researchers compared the clocks and found that the clocks that went east to west lost an average of 59 nanoseconds (a nanosecond is a billionth of a second) and those going from west to east gained an average of 273 nanoseconds.

Timekeeping

**Why did one clock gain time while the other lost it?
In fact, the answer involves speed and gravity, the
force that keeps us from flying into space.**

What if you flew on a spaceship at nearly the speed of light (186,000 miles or 300,000 kilometers per second) and made a round trip to the star Alpha Centauri. When you returned, your clock would be far behind the clocks on Earth. Nine years might have passed on Earth between the moment you left and the moment you returned, but for you the trip took only about six years. Everyone on Earth would think your clock ran slow and lost three years during the trip. But you would think the clocks on Earth ran fast and gained three years. As relativity explains, you're both correct!

While on the spaceship at near light speed, you would feel time pass at the same rate it always has. A clock would tick, tick, tick just like normal. Only after you returned home would you learn that less time passed on the spaceship than passed on Earth. If you had a twin sister who stayed on Earth during your trip, she would now be three years older than you!

THE WORLD IN MOTION

The key to relativity comes from Einstein's discovery that it's wrong to think that some objects stay in place while other objects move. Everything moves—planets orbit stars, stars orbit the center of the galaxy, and galaxies move through space. But from the point of view of each object, that object is fixed while the universe moves around it.

Who Is Moving?

If you've ever been on a train, you might have experienced the sensation of looking out the window and being unable to tell whether your train is moving forward, the train next to you is moving backward, or both trains are moving at the same time.

From Einstein's point of view, all three experiences are correct. Riders on both trains can imagine that their train is staying still while the other train is moving, and someone standing beside the tracks will say that both trains move.

An object's movement and speed make sense only when compared with other objects, and as a result time passes differently for each object.

Time is relative, but in general, we can ignore this. We live on a planet that rotates at up to 1,000 miles per hour (1,609 kilometers) and moves around the sun at 18.5 miles per second (30 kilometers). Our solar system moves through the Milky Way much faster than that and the Milky Way galaxy is moving among other nearby galaxies even faster. So it hardly matters if you drive five miles an hour faster than someone else on the highway—your wristwatches aren't precise enough to track time by nanoseconds!

To return to our spaceship example, on a round trip to Alpha Centauri you would "lose" three years when compared with everyone on Earth—but if you never returned to Earth, you'd never know that.

ACTIVITY

DAWN OF A NEW DAY

What if you had the chance to throw out the old calendars and clocks and design a completely new way to keep time? How would you do it? You might want to make July and August 80 days long so you have more time off from school, but parents and principals would probably just hold classes in the summer. You can't trick them that easily!

Keep in mind that most of our timekeeping system is arbitrary. Ancient civilizations chose something hundreds or thousands of years ago, and we still do it the same way because that's how we learned it. What if you could do anything you want? Would you still make a year equal to one revolution of the earth around the sun? A day equal to one rotation of the earth so that it again faces the sun?

Supplies

- paper
- pencil

What's important to you in a calendar or the hours of a day?

1 Try to imagine a system different from either our current one or Cupp's metric calendar. How creative can you be and still have the hours and days add up?

2 Draw your new calendar and keep track of it as the days pass, however you choose to measure your days.

3 See how well your creation works as time marches on, and don't be afraid to experiment with lots of different ideas.

GLOSSARY

altitude: how high something is above sea level.

analog: presenting data as a measurable physical quality.

anchor escapement: an escapement shaped like an anchor that made pendulum clocks much more accurate.

angle: the space between two lines that start from the same point, measured in degrees.

arc: a section of a curve or part of a circle.

archaeologist: a scientist who studies ancient people and their cultures by finding and examining things like graves, ruins, tools, and pottery.

astrolabe: a device that measures the altitude of the sun or a star to determine latitude and time.

astronomer: a person who studies the stars and planets.

atmosphere: the blanket of air surrounding the earth.

atom: a small particle of matter.

atomic clock: an extremely accurate timekeeping device that is controlled by the vibrations of atoms or molecules.

Babylonian: someone who lived in Babylon, an ancient city in what is Iraq today.

base 10 counting system: a number system based on units of 10.

base 60 counting system: a number system based on units of 60.

BCE: put after a date, BCE stands for Before the Common Era and counts down to zero. CE stands for Common Era and counts up from zero. These non-religious terms correspond to BC and AD.

cesium-133: a form of the element cesium whose vibrations are measured as a time standard.

chronometer: a very accurate timepiece, used in navigation to determine longitude.

circuit: a path for electric current to flow, beginning and ending at the same point.

circumference: the distance around the outside of a circle or globe.

civilization: a community of people that is advanced in art, science, and government.

clepsydra: a clock that uses dripping water to track time. Also called a water glass.

constellation: a group of stars visible in the night sky that form a pattern.

Curie point: the temperature at which a substance loses its magnetism.

dawn: when the sun rises above the horizon.

daylight saving time (DST): shifting the clock in the spring to gain an extra hour of daylight in the evening.

degree: a unit of measure of a circle. There are 360 degrees in a circle.

digital: presenting data as numbers.

dusk: when the sun dips below the horizon.

ellipse: an oval shape.

epagomenal day: a day outside of the regular Egyptian calendar.

equator: the imaginary line around the middle of the earth halfway between the North and South Poles.

equinox: the day in spring (March 20, 21, or 22) or fall (September 20, 21, or 22) when the number of hours of daylight and nighttime are equal everywhere in the world. The sun rises directly in the east and sets directly in the west, everywhere in the world.

GLOSSARY

escapement: a device that regulates short periods of time so they are always the same length.

evaporate: when a liquid heats up and changes to a gas.

foliot: a lever with weighted arms attached to the paddled rod of a verge escapement.

frequency: the number of times an event occurs in a specific amount of time.

fusee: a spiral pulley used to even out the power of a mainspring in a watch.

galaxy: a collection of star systems held together by gravity.

gear: a toothed wheel or cylinder that connects with another toothed part to send motion from one rotating body to another.

Global Positioning System (GPS): a system of satellites, computers, and receivers that determine the latitude and longitude of a receiver on earth by calculating the time difference for signals from different satellites to reach the receiver.

gnomon: an object that casts a shadow to keep track of the time.

grasshopper escapement: an escapement used in pendulum clocks that jumped between the teeth of a wheel.

gravity: a force that pulls objects to the earth.

Greenwich Mean Time (GMT): the solar time at the Royal Observatory in Greenwich, England, located at 0 degrees longitude.

Gregorian calendar: the calendar introduced by Pope Gregory XIII as a modification to the Julian calendar.

hertz (Hz): cycles per second.

horizon: the point in the distance where the sky and the earth (or the sea) seem to meet.

horologist: a person who makes clocks and measures time.

incense: a slow-burning wood that produces a pleasant smell when burned.

Julian calendar: the calendar created by Julius Caesar in 45 BCE.

latitude: a measure of distance from the equator, in degrees. The North Pole is 90 degrees latitude north and the South Pole is 90 degrees latitude south.

longitude: imaginary lines running from the North Pole to the South Pole around the globe.

lunar calendar: a calendar based on the phases of the moon.

lunar month: the time from one new moon to the next.

mainspring: the largest and most important spring in a watch or clock.

mannequin: a model of a person.

manufacture: to make something by machine, in a large factory.

mechanical: done automatically or as if by machine, not by a person.

mechanism: a machine or part of a machine.

millennium bug: the inability of computer software and hardware to recognize the date when it changes centuries.

millisecond: one-thousandth of a second.

molecule: a very small particle made of combinations of atoms.

navigate: to find a route to another place.

new moon: when the sun, Earth, and moon are lined up, with the moon in the middle. The side of the moon lit by the sun is facing away from Earth so the moon is not visible.

Northern Hemisphere: the half of the earth north of the equator.

orbit: the path of an object circling another object in space.

parallel: when two lines going in the same direction can go on forever and never touch, like an "=" sign.

pendulum: an object that swings freely in an arc by force of gravity

piezoelectricity: the electric current carried by quartz crystals.

portable: easily moved around.

precise: exact or detailed.

prime meridian: the imaginary line running through Greenwich, England, that divides the world into the Eastern Hemisphere and Western Hemisphere.

quadrant: an instrument used to measure the height of the planets, moon, or stars.

quasar: an object in space that emits huge amounts of energy.

radioactivity: the emission of a stream of particles or electromagnetic rays.

railway time: a standard time used by railroads that stayed the same, regardless of location.

relativity: the idea that an object's movement and speed make sense only when compared with other objects.

reservoir: a large tank or lake used to store water.

sextant: an instrument used to measure the angle between two objects.

shadow clock: a clock developed by ancient Egyptians that used the sun's shadow to track time.

sidereal day: the time it takes the earth to make one complete rotation, measured against a fixed star.

solar calendar: a calendar based on how long the earth takes to revolve around the sun.

solar day: the time it takes for the earth to make one complete rotation, measured against the sun.

Southern Hemisphere: the half of the earth south of the equator.

sundial: a tool created by the Greek inventor Anaximander (611–546 BCE) that uses a shadow cast by the sun to determine the time.

synchronize: to set watches to the same time.

telegraph: a communication system that transmits electric impulses through wires, usually in Morse code.

time zone: a region of the planet within which the same standard time is used.

Tropic of Capricorn: the line of latitude 23 degrees south of the equator.

universe: everything that exists, everywhere.

verge escapement (crown wheel): a clock escapement that uses vertical rods with paddles.

zodiac: a band of stars that includes all the planets and is divided into 12 named constellations.

RESOURCES

WEBSITES

- **Site devoted to calendar reform**
http://www.webexhibits.org/calendars/index.html

- **History of Time**
http://www.time.gov/exhibits.html

- **To find your latitude and longitude**
http://itouchmap.com/latlong.html

- **Wells Cathedral**
http://www.wellscathedral.org.uk/history/
historical-highlights/the-clock/

- **The Mariner's Museum Online**
http://ageofex.marinersmuseum.org/index.php

- **History of Olympic Timekeeping**
http://www.omegawatches.com/spirit/sports/
olympic-timekeeping

MUSEUMS & MONUMENTS

- **National Watch & Clock Museum**
http://www.nawcc.org/index.php/museumlibrary

- **Charles River Museum of Industry & Innovation**
http://www.crmi.org/exhibits/watches-clocks/

- **Royal Museums Greenwich**
http://prints.rmg.co.uk/category/8878/timekeeping

- **Cast-Iron Sidewalk Clocks, popular in the early 1900s**
http://mb.nawcc.org/showthread.php?37951-Steinway-Street-Clock-Queens-NY

- **Visit Wells Cathedral**
http://www.wellscathedral.org.uk/visit/

INDEX

Andronicus

INDEX